MEDIA CAREER GUIDE

PREPARING FOR JOBS IN THE 21ST CENTURY

EIGHTH EDITION

SHERRI HOPE CULVER

TEMPLE UNIVERSITY

JAMES SEGUIN

ROBERT MORRIS UNIVERSITY

Bedford/St. Martin's
Boston ◆ New York

For Bedford/St. Martin's

Publisher for Communication: Erika Gutierrez
Editorial Assistant: Emily Cavedon
Production Editor: Jessica Skrocki Gould
Senior Production Supervisor: Dennis J. Conroy
Marketing Manager: Adrienne Petsick
Art Direction: Lucy Krikorian
Copy Editor: Virginia Rubens
Indexer: Melanie Belkin
Cover Design: Billy Boardman
Composition: Greg Johnson/Textbook Perfect
Printing and Binding: Malloy Lithographing, Inc.

President: Joan E. Feinberg
Editorial Director: Denise B. Wydra
Director of Development: Erica T. Appel
Director of Marketing: Karen R. Soeltz
Director of Production: Susan W. Brown
Associate Director, Editorial Production: Elise S. Kaiser
Managing Editor: Shuli Traub

Library of Congress Control Number: 2011924033

Manufactured in the United States of America.

6 5 4 3 2 1
f e d c b a

For information, write: Bedford/St. Martin's, 75 Arlington Street, Boston, MA 02116 (617-399-4000)

ISBN: 978-0-312-54260-3

At the time of publication all Internet URLs published in this text were found to accurately link to their intended Web site. If you do find a broken link, please forward the information to ecavedon@bedfordstmartins.com, so that it can be corrected for the next printing.

CONTENTS

INTRODUCTION

This guidebook is for college students and recent college graduates who are interested in a career in the media/communications fields. As you begin to explore the employment track that appeals the most to your interests, it's natural to have questions about the types of jobs or careers that you can realistically look forward to securing. (Actually, it's never too early to start thinking about this.) Competition will always be intense for the most desirable jobs, and the strength of the job market will vary from year to year. In some years, the industry will be in a growth mode, and there will be plenty of jobs; in other years, the industry will be shrinking, and finding the position you want may be more difficult. For example, a 2011 job outlook survey by the National Association of Colleges and Employers stated that after several years of flat or negative hiring, employers expect to hire 13.5 percent more new grads in 2011 than in 2010.[1] Regardless of the external conditions, you should give time and energy to preparing for this important life transition. External conditions might impact *where* you look and *how*, and maybe even *what* kind of job you look for; but nothing changes the need for you to prepare well and prepare early.

Keep in mind that communications positions will always be important to the U.S. economy. Television, Internet, video games, cable, film, and advertising companies are some of our most dynamic and successful

---

[1] E. Koc, "Job Outlook 2011: College Hiring Outlook Positive in All Regions," *NACEWeb*, http://naceweb.org/Press/Releases/Job_Outlook_2011__College _Hiring_Outlook_Positive_in_All_Regions.aspx?referal=pressroom&menuid=278 (accessed October 1, 2010).

businesses. For example, in 2010, the U.S. broadcasting and cable industries saw revenue increase 6.1 percent overall after a decline in revenue in 2009.[2] In the business world, managers in both large and small corporations know that they must communicate effectively with their customers, their employees, their suppliers, and even their competitors. They must motivate, train, and inform. They must persuade, innovate, and change. All of this requires excellence in communications and employees who are visionaries, problem solvers, specialists, and technicians. It doesn't matter what position you hold in an organization today; communication skills are essential to success.

To provide you with some perspective, it's worth looking at how the Internet crossed an invisible bridge from near obscurity to stardom. Not only did this technological tool change business practices, but people worldwide found uses for the Internet in everyday life and adopted related elements—such as e-mail, smartphones, and digital MP3 players—at record speeds. The only comparable event was the development of radio and television in the early to mid-twentieth century, which led many people to create new businesses to take advantage of the new technology and consumer interest. Unfortunately, in the late twentieth century, excitement over the Internet led to the problem of overexpansion, which had dire consequences for the economy and the stock market. As a result, businesses failed, and many people lost their jobs. A few years later, the United States suffered through the terrorist attacks of September 11, 2001, which fostered additional economic problems. Today, with the fight against terrorism continuing and the slow recovery from the 2008 recession, the economy remains unsteady. College graduates who successfully navigate this economy will be those with the ability to think strategically, remain flexible, and effectively interpret trends for the future.

How can you navigate today's job market? Be willing to explore the exciting developments and intriguing possibilities that a career in media may provide. The Internet has matured and been integrated into the routines of all successful businesses. Online communications have expanded the opportunities for communications graduates, while computer technologies have continued to increase productivity. Advertising agencies, television stations, feature film companies, and even newspapers often are doing their most innovative and exciting work online.

---

[2] "One Hundred Leading Media Companies," *Advertising Age*, September 27, 2010; http://adage.com/mediaworks/article?article_id=146004 (accessed October 1, 2010).

Connections between the careers of computer programmers, Web developers, and desktop publishing specialists, on the one hand, and the careers of writers, filmmakers, editors, reporters, and photographers, on the other, are increasingly easy to see when many of us have the ability to do these activities on our home computers. By creating and uploading content online, we are increasingly acting as media *producers* in our personal lives, not just media *consumers.* Take a moment to consider the larger trend here: Whatever communications specialty interests you, you can be sure that its growth is being fed by digital and interactive technologies. Of course, a competency in technology does not make technology more important than communications skills, creativity, or the ability to work in teams. You must know your field well. However, technology skills will help you communicate more effectively and are vital in just about any forward-looking business.

More is expected of today's graduates. You are expected to be well grounded in your major *and* have the necessary technology-related skills when you graduate. Employers have always emphasized internships and job experience during college, but now these experiences are taking on greater importance than ever before. Shifts in global communication mean that foreign-language skills and experience studying abroad or in other cross-cultural environments are becoming increasingly important. Savvy college students will take these trends to heart and build solid internships and jobs into their college years. Such experiences can balance and enhance your classroom activities. When you begin interviewing for jobs, you will immediately see the value of the hours spent in a field-related internship or job. A semester spent studying abroad can also be valuable, but recruiters do not rate it as highly as an internship. If you have to choose between the two, the internship is more likely to lead directly to employment. If you do have the opportunity to travel and study overseas, be prepared to articulate to potential employers how the experience aided your ability to solve challenging problems and understand other cultures.

The vitality of the Internet has led to a cluster of jobs referred to as *interactive media, social media, digital media,* or *multimedia.* This area includes communications that are both created on and distributed through computers and intranets using new digital technologies and the Internet. New media careers typically include Web designers, content developers and directors, writers and producers of multimedia presentations, animators and graphic designers, editors of visuals and audio for streaming on the Web, and so on. Fields such as desktop publishing, digital editing, public relations, and independent filmmaking have many interactive media positions that require competence in specific software, an understanding of social media Web sites, and well-honed design skills. These careers often bridge traditional media and new media, with skills necessary from both areas. For example, public relations professionals need to know how to draft a traditional press release but also how to distribute it via the Internet and encourage viral buzz through social networks such as Facebook and Twitter. It takes a specific kind of thinking and skill to write and design for the Web, since it uses nonlinear navigation and "links" that make the experience unique. You will find more information on this topic in Chapter 1.

An advantage for communications majors is that they are often well schooled in traditional communications skills. Even in a time of heavy technology use and influence, recruiters still list having traditional communications skills (writing, speaking, presenting, and listening) as a close second to being well prepared in your discipline. Look around your classes and the places where you have worked or volunteered. Those who rise to the top are knowledgeable and motivated people who communicate well. Communicating well is followed by several other important competencies: a demonstrated ability to lead and work in teams and interpersonal and personal traits that have to do with integrity, honesty, and a positive work ethic.[3]

In our business lives, we have had the opportunity to hire young people right out of college and to see some struggle and others excel. Why the difference in performance? Surprisingly, it's easy to pinpoint. Our collective experience confirms the findings of the National Association of Colleges and Employers and the *Recruiting Trends* report by Michigan State University. Success depends on not just what you know about your field when you walk in the door. The industry will continue to change, and training can always be provided to help you learn about new software or industry trends. Employers are interested in hiring people who are flexible enough to adapt to changes—both current and unforeseen. They are interested in hiring people with a wide range of business skills and personal attributes, as discussed above. Young people who have these skills or who are willing to develop them excel in the workplace. College is the perfect place to hone these skills and attitudes. On the following pages, you will find suggestions about how to use your time in college to prepare yourself for entry into the job market. You will find detailed information about the high and low job-growth areas and

---

[3] P. Gardner et al., *Recruiting Trends 2009–2010* (East Lansing, MI: Collegiate Employment Research Institute, Michigan State University, 2006).

extensive lists of industry trade Web sites, magazines, and contact information for professional organizations. All of these resources will help you stay current with the latest developments in your field, interact with other professionals, and find a job that fits your skills and interests well.

The following chapters cross several areas—practical things that you can do, specialized reading and research, and a series of attitude checks that might require you to work on your interpersonal skills or attitudes toward work. College is the time and place to broaden your knowledge and skills, develop strong professional values, learn about your strengths and weaknesses, and begin to see how you can contribute to a better society. Whether or not you have declared a major or decided on a career direction, the ideas on the following pages can help you further define what you would like to do—and how you can succeed in reaching that goal.

1

CONSIDERING A CAREER IN MEDIA/COMMUNICATIONS

We are living in a time of revolutionary change in how we communicate and conduct our daily lives. Instead of relying solely on the familiar television set as our primary means of viewing our favorite programming, we now also "watch television" online, on our mobile phones or other touchscreen devices, through video-on-demand, or even on video billboards. We are also more likely to own the tools to create content via flip cameras, personal digital video recorders, and home editing systems. And instead of keeping such creations to ourselves, we post that content online for others to view on YouTube, Tumblr, and other video sharing Web sites. As consumers, we are enticed by these new technologies to spend more time with media and to use it in creative and innovative ways, allowing media to permeate our lives as never before. If you're considering a career in communications, this expanding media landscape presents an ever-growing range of opportunities. To help you get started, let's explore these three questions:

1. What are the trends and career opportunities in media/communications?
2. What are employers looking for?
3. Where do recruiters find qualified candidates?

WHAT ARE THE TRENDS AND CAREER OPPORTUNITIES IN MEDIA/COMMUNICATIONS?

Finding career opportunities often requires an ability to do a little trend predicting. Basically, you're trying to imagine what your preferred industry will be like when you start looking for a job after graduation—and for five to ten years afterward. How can you do that? Let's start by thinking about trends and opportunities in the communications fields that will affect the marketplace from now through 2013.

TRENDS IN MEDIA/COMMUNICATIONS

Without a doubt, the biggest trend continues to be the Internet's ever-evolving role in all things media- and communication-related. For example, the percentage of people watching videos online continues to grow. According to the marketing research company Nielsen, the mobile video audience has grown 51.2 percent since 2009, exceeding 20 million users for the first time. As you might be surprised to find out, this change is not specific to young people—55 percent of that online audience is comprised of adults aged 25 to 49, not teenagers.[1] And that number continues to climb. Nielsen also reports that more than a third of homes have a digital video recorder, up 51 percent from 2008, allowing viewers to watch TV programs on their own schedule.[2] These are important statistics for both the communications student and the communications professional. Although growth in these areas may present job opportunities, it also represents change—and such change can affect the kinds of skills that employers need, and the kinds of courses that you should consider taking while you're in school.

In addition, there are other trends in the media/communications field worth considering. One is the increase in content targeted to Hispanic audiences. Dunkin' Donuts is just one of many strong U.S. brands now producing Spanish-language commercials. Halim Trujillo, chief strategist and principal for Chicago-based Creacion Marketing Communications, states, "No matter what DMA [demographic market area] you visit, whether it's Topeka, Kansas, or Boise, Idaho, you will find at least one Hispanic radio station catering to the growing Hispanic population across the U.S."

Another trend to consider is the convergence of the traditional broadcast networks and the Internet. The networks—ABC, CBS, NBC, and Fox—continue to experience declining viewership, something likely to continue as cable and the Internet offer more diverse programming options. These networks are responding in two major ways. First, they are attempting to stay financially solid by lowering their expenses through increased production of reality programming, a genre that is less expensive to produce

---

[1] *The Nielsen Three Screen Report: Television, Internet and Mobile Usage in the U.S.*, Volume 8, Q1 2010.
[2] Ibid.

than entirely scripted shows and one that attracts audiences and ratings. Programs such as *Dancing with the Stars, Jersey Shore,* and *American Idol* exemplify this change. Second, they are using media consolidation to their advantage. As more TV and cable networks, broadband companies, radio stations, and movie studios are owned by fewer and fewer companies, their ability to promote content—whether a show, a movie, or even a book—across multiple platforms has become standard practice. A new TV show no longer premieres with a simple broadcast showing. Instead, a new TV show also simultaneously launches a Web site with related blogs and video extras, a video game featuring the show's characters, radio spots on the company-owned radio stations, original apps for mobile devices, and more. This consolidation trend can also be seen as the furthering of *media convergence,* the technological merging of content from different media into one platform. For example, content that was previously available only on its own media platform (i.e., a TV show, a book, a movie, or music) is now available from one device, a computer (or an iPad, or . . . well, stay tuned for the next big thing!).

Other examples of convergence abound. Major film studios are investing enormous sums of money to promote their films online through various Web sites—some dedicated to their product, and some that aggregate content for consumers to find in one place. The world of documentary and independent filmmaking is being transformed by digital technology. Highly portable digital cameras and editing equipment have helped enable this transformation, as have promotion and distribution through the Web and new cable and broadband channels. Some major consumer brands (such as Nike and BMW) have created Web sites showing short films, often by independent filmmakers, that indirectly or directly advertise their products. This "private label media"—premium audio and video content that has been created solely for the purpose of promoting a known brand—is just one example of how companies are attempting to reach target audiences in innovative ways through the vibrant and ubiquitous online world.[3]

All communication industries are going through enormous and exciting changes as they adapt to new technologies. Advertising agencies, TV networks, and broadband video sites are continuing to experiment with *adverblogs,* a combination of advertising and journal writing, to engage audiences in a new way. TV show characters such as Jessica Hamby from HBO's *True Blood* and Kenneth the Page from NBC's *30 Rock* post

---

[3]M. Egol, L. Moeller, and C. Vollmer, "The Promise of Private Label Media," http://www.strategy-business.com/article/09215.

video blogs to keep the audience engaged and create a deeper connection with the show. Public relations and advertising agencies are also developing projects and campaigns that use the Web in tandem with other media. For example, Old Spice created an innovative campaign using the handsome and humorous character "shirtless guy," leveraging traditional print and television commercials with the creation of 183 YouTube videos in three days, ultimately garnering 35.7 million online views. The ability to display content across multiple platforms opened up numerous creative opportunities for brand exposure as the videos went viral online.[4] According to the Interactive Advertising Bureau, all Internet ad revenue increased 7.9 percent from 2009 to a record $5.9 billion in the first quarter of 2010.[5] This is likely to continue as a major growth area over the next few years.

A common theme in these trends is that they are revamping traditional workplace patterns. For example, journalists are now being hired to write newspaper stories, report for the Web, write blogs, and appear on television news. This replaces the previous standard, which had reporters focus on just one medium. In the marketing, public relations, and advertising worlds, professionals are finding that Web communication is central to almost all their endeavors. Creative people who formerly specialized in videography are now expected to be acquainted with editing and Web streaming. This makes for a fascinating but challenging time for many.

OPPORTUNITIES IN MEDIA/COMMUNICATIONS

With the Internet's continuing evolution and other trends in the media industries, most communications fields will continue to grow, offering college graduates a wide variety of opportunities. Projections compiled by the U.S. Bureau of Labor Statistics show that public relations jobs will have faster-than-average growth (24 percent) through 2018. Those with international experience and language skills will be in even higher demand. Technical writing jobs are expected to be the fastest-growing writing and editing jobs. Film and video editing, graphic design, and advertising jobs will experience average job growth (9 to 13 percent). However, jobs that college students have often gravitated to—television news analyst, reporter, sportscaster, and weathercaster—are predicted

---

[4] J. Marshall, "Old Spice Campaign Generated 35 Million Video Views in Seven Days," July 19, 2010, http://www.clickz.com/clickz/news/1724682/old-spice-campaign-generated-35-million-video-views-seven-days (accessed August 22, 2010).

[5] "Internet Advertising Revenues Hit $5.9 Billion in Q1 '10, Highest First-Quarter Revenue Level on Record," http://www.iab.net/about_the_iab/recent_press_releases/press_release_archive/press_release/pr-051310 (accessed August 12, 2010).

to decline over the next ten years, in part due to consolidation and con-vergence in the industry.[6] Generally, you will find fewer opportunities with local television and radio stations, particularly for on-air positions.

Opportunities to work in media/communications may be found everywhere. However, they will vary greatly depending on which geo-graphic region you search in and whether your preference is to work for a local, national, or global company.

Start by thinking about your possibilities from a regional perspective. Consider midsize cities such as Birmingham, Alabama; Toledo, Ohio; Boulder, Colorado; or San Bernardino, California. Each has numer-ous communications companies such as online ventures, in addition to television, cable, and radio stations. You can also find dozens of com-munications suppliers, mostly small companies and freelancers who are creating communications for different purposes. If you look within a fifty-mile radius of almost any city, you will find that hundreds of com-munications firms exist. Go to smaller city markets, and you will con-tinue to find opportunities. Such companies exist in almost every city, and many are doing innovative work. After all, whether the economy is on an upswing or a downswing, companies still need communications services. To get a better sense of the opportunities that exist, explore a few corporations of different sizes in a given area.

You can be sure that some departments within a company are produc-ing communications that are distributed internally and externally. You can also be sure that there are a bevy of small creative firms and freelanc-ers providing communications services regularly for this company. If the firm is growing, then the communications services are growing, too. It doesn't matter what the company does. Whether it's part of the manu-facturing or service industries, it must communicate to stay in business. Often such entities use a wide variety of communications and media to get their messages to target audiences. Companies are also *outsourcing*, hiring companies outside their own firms, for more of their communica-tions work. This creates a dynamic and highly competitive market to sup-ply services. Typical firms producing corporate work include advertising and public relations, video production, Web development, graphic de-sign, technical writing, still photography, marketing, multimedia, new media, and training and development.

But are these firms healthy and in a hiring mood? Michigan State University's *Recruiting Trends 2009–2010* predicts a decline in the hir-

---

[6] U.S. Bureau of Labor Statistics, *Occupational Outlook Handbook* (Washington, D.C.: U.S. Government Printing Office, 2005), http://www.bls.gov.

ing of college graduates in 2011 of between 7 and 12 percent over the previous year on a national level. However, it is estimated that some categories of communications companies (i.e., interactive media, public relations, and advertising/sales) are expected to increase 3 to 4 percent. According to *Recruiting Trends*, the South Central region of the United States will have the largest increase in hiring of graduates with bachelor's degrees, employing up to 6 percent new labor. This is followed by the Northeast and Southwest regions at 3 percent each. Most other regions will see a slight decline.[7] *Recruiting Trends 2009–2010* also shows average salaries in some communications fields (see Table 1.1).

Table 1.1 Average Starting Salaries, 2009–2010

Selected Salaries		Selected Bachelors	
All Associates	$36,200	Accounting	$41,300
All Bachelors	$39,900	Finance	$42,200
MBA	$56,800	Marketing	$38,300
Accounting (MS)	$49,100	Supply Chain	$41,500
Engineering (MS)	$58,600	Advertising	$35,500
Computer Science (MS)	$57,100	Computer Science	$47,500
Engineering (PhD)	$68,900	Chemical Engineering	$50,000
		Civil Engineering	$47,600
		Electrical Engineering	$51,600
		Mechanical Engineering	$51,100
		Nursing	$42,300
		Mathematics	$43,600
		Psychology	$36,400
		Agriculture	$37,300

Source: Recruiting Trends 2009–2010, http://www.ceri.msu.edu/recruiting-trends/

WHAT ARE EMPLOYERS LOOKING FOR?

If you are wondering whether you will be qualified to enter a job market that seems to be changing rapidly and demanding more and more from college graduates, let's consider what employers say they're looking for in graduates. If you are majoring in communications, you are probably in a liberal arts program. Your college or university most likely

---

[7]Michigan State University, "Recruiting Trends 2009–2010," http://www.ceri .msu.edu/recruiting-trends/ (accessed August 19, 2010).

ON THE JOB: Be Prepared

[An ideal candidate] does his/her homework, knows what the project is, comes in with IDEAS about how they can help the project, and shows tremendous enthusiasm and a point of view about the project.

Bob Kirsh
Executive Producer,
cable television series

has a core set of required general courses that cross economics, science, math, information systems, history, social sciences, and other departments. If this is true for you, be glad because recruiters say they want well-rounded individuals with expertise beyond just a specific technology or set of technologies.

In this age of the Internet and media convergence, you might expect that companies want only technological wizards. If you are technologically advanced, that's great, but it is not enough. Companies value well-rounded, flexible people because in the long run they are better at strategic planning, problem solving, and learning new technologies as they are created. According to *Recruiting Trends 2009–2010*, the message for college graduates is that they must be "focused, directed and connected." Recruiters are seeking college graduates with extraordinary critical thinking skills, communication skills, leadership, initiative, and an innovative spirit. This list of qualities from the Michigan State University study becomes even more powerful when we compare it with the Job Outlook 2010 study by the National Association of Colleges and Employers (NACE). Communications skills lead their list and are followed by analytical skills, the ability to work in a team, technical skills, and a strong work ethic. However, the study also notes that these skills will not make up for a poor GPA (grade point average) or lack of experience with a variety of employers.[8] If you feel that you are lacking in any of these areas, use your college days wisely to take courses that

---

[8] National Association of Colleges and Employers (NACE), "Employers Rank Communication Skills First Among Job Candidate Skills and Qualities," http://www.naceweb.org/Press/Releases/Employers_Rank_Communication_Skills_First_Among_Job_Candidate_Skills_and_Qualities_%281-21-10%29.aspx (accessed August 19, 2010).

improve your communication skills and writing skills. Apply for internships where you can put these skills to work and learn about the realities of the workplace.

Since most new media communications are created using specialized computer software programs, graduates in this area have what many employers are looking for. No matter where you look in the communications fields, employers have an insatiable need for graduates with technical expertise. Newspapers want graduates who understand journalism and Web technologies. Writers who know desktop publishing are in greater demand than those who don't. Competent video and television program editors who can work as "preditors" (producer and editor) are employable; those who cannot will have trouble finding a producing or editing job. In many ways, the interactive and new media field represents what is happening throughout the communications industries—a melding of traditional media skills with software competence or technical expertise. For many students, success in the job market will come because they developed communications and technical expertise while in college.

WHERE DO RECRUITERS FIND QUALIFIED CANDIDATES?

Recruiters have one goal in mind—to find the most qualified candidate as quickly as possible; and they prefer to find this candidate using the least expensive method possible. This means that they prefer to find the candidate through word-of-mouth referrals (costing nothing) rather than placing ads on specialty Web sites. The findings from *Recruiting Trends 2009–2010* support this preference. This report states that the most popular recruiting strategies used on campus are co-ops/internships and college fairs, followed by resumé requests, campus visits, faculty referrals, and last, on-campus interviews. Beyond campus recruiting, the most frequent methods mentioned for recruiting are a referral from a current employee, postings on national Web sites, and social media. With many of these options, you have the responsibility of seeking job information online or cultivating contacts and networking with people who can help put your name in front of the person doing the hiring. Note, also, that most of these options cost employers little or nothing.

Although recruiters are a pivotal contact point for many students, be warned that focusing exclusively on recruiters ignores a wide range of other people who are responsible for filling jobs. In many companies, job openings are handled by an associate or manager in the human resources department. This person often acts as a liaison between a potential candidate and the manager to whom the new hire will be reporting. HR employees draft job descriptions, screen resumés, conduct pre-interviews, negotiate salary offers, and often narrow down the pool of candidates to the four or five who meet directly with the supervisor. In small companies, all of these responsibilities are handled directly by the manager to whom you will be reporting. How does that change the recruiting process? Well, hiring the right person for a job is vitally important, but managers who are responsible for running a department often have little time to devote to this critical task. Such managers, even more than recruiters, need to find a candidate quickly and efficiently. This is why internships and co-ops are fertile hiring grounds. For a busy manager, interns are the perfect candidates; they require no searching to find and no cost to recruit.

Job and career fairs are worthwhile, but you may find that few job fairs focus on jobs with media and communication companies. Be on the lookout for job fairs that are sponsored by local or regional professional associations in media and communications. A few of those associations are

- National Television Academy
- Public Relations Association
- Broadcast Pioneers
- National Cable Television Association
- Women in Communications

One final thought for the adventurous: Even though the United States is the largest producer—and consumer—of communications in the world, there are exciting opportunities overseas as U.S. companies continue to expand into South America, Europe, Asia, and beyond. If you haven't already, you should consider taking a semester to study abroad. Many colleges and universities offer opportunities for foreign study, and the global experience can help when the time comes to find a job. If your college or university does not offer such a program, consider enrolling through another school; the credits are often transferable.

2

WHERE THE JOBS ARE

Jobs in the media and communications fields are numerous and wide ranging. Throw out any assumption that you might have about what jobs are available. Almost any business-related job that you can think of, from attorney to youth worker, may be found in a media company. Growth in media industries—including social media, video gaming, and other new media areas—means that new jobs, new titles, and new positions are being created, even at established media companies.

Opportunities abound, but many are tucked away under job categories that don't belong to the established media and communications job market. Jobs may be found within corporate communications, education, new media, public information (government), training and development, satellite communications, and video games/simulations, in addition to the more commonly considered fields of television, radio, music, newspapers, and so on. Many of these new jobs are similar to those in established communications fields. Widen your horizons and you may open the door to twice as many opportunities as you originally thought you had.

One of your first decisions will be whether to search for a position in a large company or a small company (for this book, a small company is one with fewer than fifty employees). Everything from job responsibilities, job title, office space, types of projects, and salary can be different in a small company as opposed to a large one. In a small media company, managers are more likely to brainstorm *with* the creative team, go out on a sales call, or personally fix equipment—especially if that's the job they held *before* they became a manager. In a large media company, a manager is likely to be removed from those kinds of tasks because the company employs specialists for each area and maintains a strict division of labor. And if there are active labor unions at the company, you will find job responsibilities well defined.

There are differences in workload and type of work as well. Large companies may provide you with experience on more complex, prestigious projects and often can afford to pay higher salaries and better benefits. Small companies are likely to have a more informal atmosphere and to make up for lower salaries with the opportunity to be involved in or learn about other areas of the company. There are advantages and disadvantages to each, but you should be aware of the differences so that you can choose the environment in which you are most comfortable. Internships and part-time or freelance work are excellent ways to experience the differences between the working conditions and expectations of large and small companies before accepting a full-time position.

SIX COMMON MEDIA JOB TYPES

Jobs in the media and communications fields can be divided into six job types—management, sales, creative, technical, finance, and legal—that are found in nearly every media business, but the specific titles and responsibilities vary greatly. Job titles often follow a hierarchy in wording. Lower-level supervisory positions often include the word *manager* (such as *promotions manager*). More responsibility may be reflected by the word *director* included in the title (such as *director of sales*). Increased responsibility may be reflected by a *vice president* title or even *executive* or *senior vice president* (such as *vice president of online content*). These titles will vary in different companies, but they are often your first clue to the level of responsibility that is expected in a particular position. Following are brief descriptions of these six job types and the job titles or positions they include.

Management positions include *department heads, vice presidents, presidents, chief executive officers,* and *chief financial officers.* (See additional titles in the paragraph above.) These are generally positions in which a central function of the job is supervising other people or a team. These jobs typically require prior management experience and demonstrated competence, since the health of the organization is directly related to the vision and leadership of its management. Since the work of a media or communications company is often centered on teams, project-based (such as advertising campaigns, television programs, magazine issues, or radio shows), and done on tight deadlines, managers must be adept at supervising small groups and solving problems quickly. Management styles that allow for flexibility and creativity yet still provide the leadership to drive projects forward are typical of successful media managers.

Sales positions involve directly seeking and securing revenue for the company. In media companies, the salesperson is usually called an *account executive* or *account representative* because the job involves securing the initial sale and maintaining the relationship with the "customer," "client," or "account." In a small company, the account executive may be responsible for researching and calling on new prospects, drafting sales proposals and "media buys," doing sales presentations, working with clients on their advertising copy or graphics, and even making sure that the client pays on time. In a large company, a sales team that includes a *sales assistant, research assistant,* and *media planner* may assist with several of these duties. A *sales manager* will work with individual *account executives* to help them achieve the company's sales goals. In a national company, there may be a *regional sales manager* and a *national sales manager.* Marketing, sales, and promotions responsibilities are often linked, but they are three different specialties: *marketing* focuses on analyzing target audiences and strategically positioning the product or service; *sales* is based on direct interaction with clients and on raising money; and *promotions* work draws attention to an organization or a product through special events, contests, outreach activities, and giveaways.

It is worth noting that you'll rarely hear the term *sales* in the nonprofit or public broadcasting/media industries. In those businesses, the department responsible for raising money is known as *development,* and the salespeople or account executives are generally known as *underwriting representatives.*

Creative positions involve the design and execution of any print, electronic, or computer communication or content. *Programming, promotion, production, marketing,* and *editorial* are names of departments using creative employees such as *writers, producers, animators,* and *designers.* Creative people often work on teams with *project managers* so that the elements of a project can move ahead on schedule, on budget, and in an orderly manner. Most media companies contain many creative professionals in several departments. Job titles are numerous, but here's a list of some of the most common: *videographer, producer, director, graphic designer, publicist, marketing associate, news reporter, speech writer, production assistant,* DJ (*disk jockey*), *on-air talent, casting director,* and *scriptwriter.*

Technical positions involve the maintenance of equipment and coordination of the proper technologies with projects so that communications work can be planned, produced, distributed, and consumed. Video editing equipment may have to be reconfigured or relocated from project to project, satellite time must be scheduled, computers may have to be installed and set up with software, and so on. Technology is particularly important to the production and distribution of communications, but it is involved in all phases of the business. Job titles include *master control operator, IT (Internet technology) specialist,* and *engineer.*

Some positions, such as *editor, videographer,* and *video game developer,* involve equal parts technical skills *and* creative skills. A person holding one of these positions must have expertise in the use of the equipment central to that job, as well as the creative abilities needed to produce content.

Finance positions deal directly with the intake of money to the business and the reporting that is necessary to keep track of financial data. In a small or medium-size company, people in financial positions often manage employee benefits (such as health care and savings plans), employee salary negotiations, and annual reviews. There is nothing inherently different about financial positions in a media company as opposed to other businesses, but these positions are separate from the other categories listed. Job titles include *bookkeeper, accountant, chief financial officer, payroll manager, accounts receivable manager,* and *human resources manager.*

Legal positions are typically found only in large media and communication companies. Legal issues for small companies may be handled by hiring an outside law firm (although large companies may also elect to handle their needs through an outside firm). These positions have mainly two roles—*attorney* and *paralegal* or *legal assistant.* Employees may handle contracts between the media company and outside vendors or producers, ensure compliance with industry regulatory policies, and negotiate key employment contracts.

Now that you have a feel for the job *types,* let's delve more deeply into the industries and job areas. The following list of media and communication industries and related industries is worth considering:

Media and Communication Industries
1. Advertising
2. Animation/graphic arts
3. Audio production
4. Book publishing
5. Commercials (advertising) production
6. Feature, documentary, and independent film production

7. Magazine publishing
8. Music/recording production
9. New media/Web-based media/multimedia
10. Newspaper publishing/journalism
11. Public relations
12. Radio
13. Social media/interactive media
14. Television: broadcast and cable
15. Video games
16. Video production
17. Writing

Related Industries

1. Arts/theater management
2. Captioning for the hearing impaired
3. Consulting
4. Distribution and duplication
5. Education: crisis communications, media training, teaching, conducting workshops and seminars
6. Equipment and business brokers
7. Equipment manufacturers and suppliers
8. Institutional communications (nonbroadcast): includes communications/media created by corporations, colleges/universities, government, military, and nonprofit organizations
9. Language translation services
10. Law: media and entertainment
11. Marketing and sales
12. Media/communications facilities design and installation
13. Political communications
14. Professional and trade organizations
15. Research: audience analysis, business, library, film, and video and film stock libraries
16. Rides/simulations: amusement parks, museums, science centers
17. Satellite related: direct broadcast satellite, video conferencing
18. Still photography
19. Talent: actors, newscasters and weathercasters, on-camera spokespeople, and voice-over narrators
20. Trade magazines and Web sites, newsweeklies, publications, awards, conferences, and marketplaces
21. Training and development

EIGHT COMMON MEDIA BUSINESS AREAS

Now we will take a brief look at some of the typical jobs that are found in eight common media/communications business areas. There are many more positions than can be covered here, but this list gives you an idea of the types of jobs that are available and the job responsibilities that go with the titles. You will find similar positions in the other communications industries not mentioned in this section. More detailed information can be found in the references listed in the Additional Resources section at the end of this book.*

ADVERTISING

Account Executive. Oversees accounts with agency clients so that advertising campaigns are creatively and efficiently managed. The account executive is a liaison between client and agency who works to keep both the client and the agency happy. This is a position with high visibility on both the agency level and the community level.

*Senior Producer. Coordinates activities with outside production firms that produce commercials and other creative work. This person identifies various directors who specialize in shooting and directing commercials, collects bid packets from directors and production houses that are vying to work on a campaign, sets up call times and production details with directors contracted by an agency, and oversees the production of the commercial.

Media Buyer. Contacts media outlets (such as TV stations, magazines, and Web sites) to purchase air time, banner ads, or other space for clients' advertising and negotiates pricing with those media. This position combines both statistical analysis *and* deal negotiation.

*Production Manager. Coordinates and schedules the activities with outside production houses that the agency contracts with, such as studio time and audio production facilities for voice-overs. This person juggles many projects at once and coordinates with both outside companies and in-house agency people to ensure that the work is properly completed. The production manager must understand all phases of advertising production.

Product Wrangler. Coordinates integrated marketing (product placement) in media, such as in films or on television shows.

---

* Note: All positions that begin with an asterisk may also be found in other types of media companies. For example, public relations agencies have a structure that is similar to that of advertising agencies, and many of the jobs in both businesses have similar titles.

Art Director. Oversees the design of graphics, Web sites, animation, signage, shelfcards, the "look" of television commercials, and so on. This person attends still-photo shoots and film or video productions for commercials. He or she works closely with the creative people hired by an agency so that the agency achieves the content and creative goals planned in the campaign.

Copy Writer. Writes radio, television, print, or online advertising copy. Scripts are submitted for approval to clients, and changes are common. Creativity, the ability to write quickly, the ability to communicate effectively with few words, and knowledge of script-writing software are prerequisites for this job.

Artist/Designer. Draws or uses computer software to create graphics and images for advertising art, animatics (first-draft storyboards for commercials), production storyboards, new business presentation art, print layouts, and Web pages.

Assistant Positions. Many departments have jobs with the word *assistant* in the title, and in most cases these jobs are beginning-level positions. The job responsibilities depend on the experience and ability of the individual. These jobs provide opportunities for beginners to learn many aspects of the advertising business. Typical assistant positions are *media assistant, production assistant, advertising assistant, marketing assistant,* and *assistant copy writer.*

INSTITUTIONAL COMMUNICATIONS AND TRAINING (CORPORATE, GOVERNMENT, NONPROFITS)

Director of Communications. Oversees the many facets of corporate communications, including creating strategic branding messages and providing information about the institution to the press in the form of press releases, video news releases, press conferences, or brochures. This position typically directs a staff that is responsible for creating and distributing those materials and oversees the hiring and supervision of freelance artists, designers, photographers, videographers, writers, and various printing and production companies.

Director of Media Relations. Handles inquiries from reporters or producers from news and entertainment outlets, such as newspapers, magazines, television/cable programs, radio shows, and online sites. This person promotes stories, events, products, or services to the media. He or she often interfaces with the media during a crisis or negative situation.

Desktop Publishing Specialist. Combines text, visuals, and design elements to create brochures and a wide variety of other documents for internal and external use by the company.

Writer. Writes a wide variety of communications—annual reports, press releases, press kits, brochures, in-house newsletters, videos, multimedia, promotional and sales materials, trade-show and meeting materials, new business pitches, responses to customers, technical documents, Web site content, and training materials.

Speech Writer. Researches and writes speeches for top-level management.

Graphic Artist or Designer. Develops and executes the layout and artistic treatment for a variety of materials for use in all communications, including the design for trade-show kiosks and sales areas. May be involved in many of the items listed for writers, including videos, newsletters, technical communications, and so on.

Camera Operator/Videographer. Uses a creative viewpoint and technical skill to record scenes. The individual in this position may also be responsible for directing talent, carrying equipment, interacting with clients, and overseeing lighting.

Technical Engineer. Participates in the selection, installation, and maintenance of audio, video, computer, and transmission equipment and facilities.

Training Specialist. Plans, organizes, directs, and delivers a wide range of training programs, often developing the materials needed in addition to providing the training. For example, training specialists might conduct orientation sessions or programs on health benefits and retirement programs. Often these programs use a variety of media delivered through computers and video.

Video/Multimedia Editor. Edits various visual communications. This person is usually familiar with sophisticated digital editing equipment.

MAGAZINE PUBLISHING

Publisher. Supervises all activities of the magazine from production to circulation. The publisher sets the editorial policy and oversees financial operations.

Managing Editor. Oversees the editorial and production departments to maintain quality and meet deadlines.

Staff Writer. Writes features or columns, usually in a particular content area—politics, gardening, or the computer industry, for example.

Copy Editor. Edits and proofreads all text to ensure that content is accurate and grammatically correct.

Editorial Assistant. Entry-level position that provides a variety of administrative functions, including typing, filing, data entry, proofreading, and rewriting.

Art Director. Supervises the development and execution of art that is required for the production of the magazine.

Assistant to the Art Director/Artist. Creates and designs graphics and page layouts in preparation for printing.

Sales Representative. Makes presentations to clients to sell advertising space. The sales representative interacts with clients to ensure they are pleased with the results of the advertising project.

Circulation/Subscription Manager. Supervises the planning and financial operations of subscription and newsstand sales.

NEW MEDIA/WEB-BASED MEDIA/MULTIMEDIA

*Consultant. Provides assistance on a "per project" basis. Many new business ventures begin when individual consulting jobs increase and it becomes clear that an opportunity exists to develop a full-fledged business. May provide assistance in financial management, strategic planning, marketing, or technology assessment.

Content Director. Seeks appropriate material for the target audience of the project by coordinating the content (making sure it all works together) and aligning it to a particular perspective or theme.

Designer. Provides graphic design and other artistic services for content providers.

Director. Directs the recording of visuals, audio, and other media so that they will meet the specific needs of a new media project, such as an online sales presentation.

Producer. Plans, budgets, schedules, and oversees all creative components of a media project. The producer is usually responsible for hiring the rest of the production team.

Programmer. Develops proprietary content or computer applications for a particular site.

Software Developer. Develops applications, or "apps," for computer use.

Web Master. Oversees all facets of a particular Web site. May supervise a team of designers and content providers or handle those responsibilities personally.

Writer. Creates concepts and writes scripts for Web-based, interactive, or multimedia presentations.

RADIO INDUSTRY

Station/General Manager. Supervises all staff, develops station policies, oversees department budgets, keeps current with government and Federal Communications Commission regulations, and acts as a liaison to the community. The station manager handles all day-to-day operations and reports to either a station group owner or network.

New Business Development Director. Develops partnerships with outside companies or organizations to create new methods of generating revenue.

Account Executive. Sells advertising time, maintains a positive relationship with clients and potential clients, studies market analyses, and writes and makes sales presentations.

National Sales Manager. Coordinates national accounts with the local station for advertising. May also secure advertising from national companies when they are headquartered in the local market.

News Reporter/Writer. Develops, researches, and writes stories on breaking news or feature topics. Utilizes news gathered from field operations or news wire services.

Promotions Director. Works to differentiate the station from competitors, gain new listeners, and promote the station and on-air personalities by developing special events, contests, and other outreach activities.

Public Affairs Director. Oversees the production of public service announcements and public service programming meant to serve the non-profit sector and community issues.

Traffic/Continuity Manager. Prepares the daily log that specifies exactly when all elements of the program schedule (including features, commercials, and public service announcements) will air and ensures correct copy in all announcements. Duties may be handled by one person or separated into two or more positions, depending on the size of the station.

Copy Writer. Creates concepts and writes copy for commercials, promotions, public service announcements, and other station needs.

Production Director. Oversees all technical elements of commercials, promos, and other content. Records and mixes production elements (such as voice, music, and effects), oversees dubbing, works with clients, and may write some of the material.

On-Air Talent. Acts as host or reporter for programs and other content. May be hired to fill a specific on-air time slot, to report news, or to record voice-overs for commercials and promotions. May also act as production director for this work.

Chief Engineer. Participates in the purchase, installation, and repair of equipment; ensures that the station operates within proper technical standards; sets up remote broadcasts; and coordinates activities with the programming department.

Producer/Radio Show. Books guests, coordinates schedules, plans remote (out-of-station) broadcasts, suggests or manages Web-based content, manages on-air talent, keeps track of time cues, and handles all elements that are necessary to keep the show running smoothly.

Sales Assistant. Enters new sales orders, works on proposals, and assists in the day-to-day operations of the sales department.

Engineering Assistant. Assists with computers, software, and broadcast equipment maintenance.

TELEVISION INDUSTRY

General Manager/Station Manager. Supervises all staff, develops station policies, oversees department budgets, keeps current with government and Federal Communications Commission regulations, and acts as a liaison to the community. The station manager handles all day-to-day operations and reports to either a station group owner or network.

Sales Manager. Supervises all sales representatives and ensures that the team is securing the revenue targets that are put forth by the station's general manager.

Account Executive. Sells air time and/or Web-based advertising, such as banner ads. Makes presentations, works with clients, and develops relationships with new clients to raise revenue for the station. Acts as a liaison between the station and the advertiser.

ON THE JOB: Professionalism from Start to Finish

Six important tips for interviewing with a television network: (1) Watch the channel, visit the Web site, study the schedule, look at the graphics, work out the strategy. (2) Have something interesting to say about #1. (3) Be passionate. (4) Don't try to negotiate a salary. (5) Remember the name of the person interviewing you. (6) Follow up with a handwritten note the same or following day of the interview.

Andrew Beecham
Vice President Programming,
cable network

Program Director. Acquires content and creates a program schedule to attract and increase a target audience. May supervise the production of original station programming. Responsible for budgeting acquisitions so that both ratings and profits grow. May work with a programming assistant or other programming staff.

Promotions Director. Develops and executes a strategy to differentiate the station from the competition and to persuade new viewers to watch more. May use on-air promotional announcements, Web-based contests, events, press releases, and other public relations elements.

Producer. Manages all production elements of a television program or series of programs. The producer is responsible for content, style, production flow, and budgeting and hires the team that is necessary to handle those elements.

Studio Director. Establishes camera positions and shot sequences for in-studio productions. Blocks scripts (determining camera placement and movement during particular words or stories), works with talent, oversees lighting, and takes responsibility for the look of the program. For programs recorded at remote locations (such as a sports event), the director might work from a remote vehicle to accomplish many of the same operations.

Technical Director (T.D.). Operates the equipment that selects camera shots and special effects (known as the *switcher*), as instructed by the director during a studio or remote broadcast. Depending on the facility set-up or size of the production, the director may serve as his or her own T.D.

Engineer. Ensures that equipment is in place and functioning properly for required broadcast and cable standards and needs of the production team.

Production Assistant. Assists the producer and the production team with administrative and other needs. An entry-level position.

On-Air Talent. Acts as news anchor or field reporter, records voice-overs, hosts special programs, and attends community events as a station representative.

News Producer. Gathers the team to write, shoot, voice-over, and edit news packages and feature stories for news broadcasts or online news sites. May operate as a crew of one—or several (camera operator, sound engineer, and reporter), depending on the shooting environment and budget of the media operation.

Preditor. Acts as a one-person production center, serving as producer, shooter, *and* editor. ("Preditor" combines "producer" and "editor.") This is a relatively new job title influenced by technological advancements, shrinking production budgets, and tighter production schedules.

News Director. Supervises all aspects of a news operation, including reporters, camera operators, anchors, and writers to ensure editorial competency and a growing audience.

Newscast Producer. Determines the overall content and story flow of a particular newscast. Responsible for creating a professional and accurate news program.

Editor. Edits field or studio-recorded elements or elements downlinked from satellites, downloaded from Web sites, and other sources into news stories. Adds voice-overs, graphics, and music when appropriate.

News Writer. Writes news-length stories for specific newscasts, in-depth news specials, and related programming as assigned.

Graphic Artist. Creates computer-generated art for news, commercials, promotions, Web sites, and other needs.

Floor Manager. Acts as a liaison between the director, on-air talent, and studio personnel during a studio production.

Web Content Manager. Develops content specifically for Web-based environments. May provide the online source for content previously aired, may provide original content, or may manage user-generated content (such as material the audience generated and uploaded).

VIDEO GAMES

Game Developer. Develops new concepts and articulates navigation and activity flow for video games. Utilizes current trends and state-of-the-art technology to influence game structure.

3D Animator. Develops and creates three-dimensional graphics and animation for use in games.

Production Manager. Oversees any live production necessary, as well as development of art components, animation, and compositing to keep the production on time and on budget.

Computer Programmer. Develops and writes the technical coding as necessary to execute the concept of the game developer. May work with the developer as a team in creating the game.

Marketing/Public Relations Director. Develops concepts and creative methods for reaching potential consumers. Often, video game companies are very small companies (under ten people), and many different communications functions are handled by one person. This position interacts with vendors, the media, and customers to promote the company and its products.

Account Executive. Encourages retail outlets, educational distributors, and other market segments to purchase or carry the product line or game. For an online game, the account executive may solicit advertisers for banner ads or other revenue-producing method.

VIDEO PRODUCTION COMPANY

Producer. Manages the production of a media product from beginning to end, ensuring that the production is completed on time, on budget, and with a high level of creativity.

Director. Provides leadership for all elements included in the creation of the visuals and creative vision for a production. Blocks scripts for shooting, works with talent, determines shot composition, and oversees lighting. Directors often work as freelancers, moving from project to project or production company to production company. Directors often specialize in a particular genre or media, such as commercials, industrials, webisodes, multicamera programs, sports, or soap operas.

Production Manager. Coordinates and schedules all elements of a client's project, including preproduction, production, and postproduction.

Camera Operator. Records material digitally, on videotape, or on film for clients. Also referred to as a *shooter,* many also act as the director when doing smaller budget jobs or shooting nonbroadcast work, such as industrial videos.

Sound Designer. Coordinates and records music, voice-overs, and sound effects for projects. May also act as audio engineer and select and set up audio equipment required for different projects.

Graphic Artist/Animation Artist. Creates still and moving images for use in commercials, institutional videos, television/cable programs, DVDs, and Web pages using computer-based technology.

Account Executive. Drafts proposals, makes presentations to clients about the quality of the production team and services, and negotiates production budgets and other elements to gain production-work clients.

Writer. Writes scripts for institutional videos, public service announcements, and commercials utilizing creative approaches based on a client's stated goals and needs.

Note: Audio production facilities have a business structure and work flow that is similar to those of video production companies. Those who are interested in music production and the recording of voice-over narration should look into this vibrant part of the industry.

3

PREPARING FOR A CAREER IN MEDIA

The following four chapters (Chapters 3, 4, 5, and 6) provide useful tips to help you prepare for a career in media/communications. Some of these suggestions require hands-on work, others require learning new skills, and still others are more interpersonal. Select just a few tips to begin with. Start slowly, and build on your successes. As you move through your college years, your interests may change. Career interests often become more specific during this time. All of a sudden, you will find yourself omitting certain kinds of jobs from your list and focusing on others. With each decision, you're closer to knowing what you want to do and how to succeed at doing it.

Rather than wait to begin your career search with all the other graduating seniors, consider getting started now. Early preparation can lead to early success. This chapter lists twelve different tips to help you start your quest for a job in media/communications. These are items that benefit from advance planning, either because they simply cannot be done with two days' notice or because they lead to actions and habits that you need to develop over time.

1. START CAREER PLANNING EARLY

It's reasonable to start career planning during your sophomore year. Consider your first year in college and the summer following it as a time of adjustment. After that, it's time to get a little more serious about career preparation—and each year afterward, a little more serious still. It's okay to start slowly, and it doesn't matter if you have little idea of what you want to do. Everything suggested in this guidebook will help you focus your ideas and gain direction.

When you take action, unexpected things happen. For example, you may go to a bookstore to find a certain book but instead find a different book or run into someone who ends up helping you much more. These incidents occur frequently for those who keep trying. There is only one action that you don't want to take—no action. (Remember, not making a decision *is* a decision.) A delay in action will delay your preparation and prevent you from developing your particular interests and passions—which, if you have none now, will come in time if you work at acquiring them. Without a strong area of interest and a developing devotion to it, you will not be motivated to learn more and seek out new experiences and opportunities.

Early career planning is serious business because out of these new learning opportunities and experiences—many of which come by chance—will come a direction that will shape your life after college. Awaiting you just a few years away may be a whole new set of friends, a much different location, and job responsibilities that you can't imagine right now. Envision where you want to be, try to visualize your situation, and then work toward it step by step. College is an engaging, mind-broadening learning experience. Make it pay off for you.

2. KEEP A NOTEBOOK OR JOURNAL

News reports, blogs, magazines, and books often tell stories about successful people whose initial ideas were jotted down on a notepad or napkin and later sold for millions. (One of the enduring myths of the Harry Potter series is that J. K. Rowling jotted her initial idea for the books on a napkin!) If you are careful, this could be a valuable practice for you in the future, so get into the habit now by keeping a file or notebook where you write down the ideas, themes, people, organizations, events, or items that matter to you.

In addition to ideas, a personal notebook can help you keep track of what you are learning. Notebook entries aren't directed by potential test questions or assignments; they're about you and the things that you deem important. After a year of making entries, you may find when you look back through them that they remind you of some important experiences you had forgotten. This points out one value of a journal: It helps you track your progress. This alone may boost your self-confidence and help you define a direction. A notebook can be the glue that holds together different thoughts, such as the names of people who've inspired you—teachers, classroom guest speakers, people interviewed in the media, authors. The same holds true for organizations that impress you—places where you could perhaps see yourself working. Events that you attend and books that you read qualify as well. What you note will probably depend on the time that you have available and your motivation. If you make the time to keep a journal, you will find it to be more helpful than you can imagine.

3. BE A CRITICAL CONSUMER

It is said that film director Steven Spielberg watched the movie *2001: A Space Odyssey* (1968) hundreds of times when he was a young man. We don't know if this is true, but think about it for a moment: watching one film over and over again until there is nothing else to learn from it. Have you ever done that? Did you ever like a song so much that you played it over and over again, each time noticing a new lyric or instrument and finding nuances you didn't catch at first? Media and communications can go by us so rapidly that often we don't have time to study them. Because of that, we encourage you to try another approach—and it doesn't matter what communications field interests you most. Find the best communications in your field—the ones that the professional community recognizes as being of highest quality—and then study each one individually and in a concentrated fashion. Read, watch, and listen to these communications again and again. Outline their structure, listing their strong and weak points. Keep a journal of what you are learning from them. Ask yourself why and how the authors or creators achieved what they did. How did they go about creating that communication? You may discover unexpected insights. If you find yourself lost, it's a clear indication of what you need to learn in your college coursework or on your own.

Another action you can take—and it's easy—is to pay attention to current communications in your specialty. If your interest is in independent films and documentaries, for example, you should allow yourself enough time to download them from independent broadband sites, watch them on HBO, or view them wherever else they may appear. Often, you can find film festivals or film houses that show independent films. You should know where they are and make it a goal to see what they're showing. If your interest is in advertising, you should view and critically analyze ads everywhere you see or hear them—from billboards and magazines to television, radio, and the Web. There's so much advertising around us that you won't have to change your schedule; just start taking advantage of what you find naturally in your day-to-day activities.

Whether or not you follow up on any of this probably comes down to one question: How badly do you want to succeed? Those who are hungry, driven, or committed will take advantage of learning opportunities, and such efforts will pay off. Success takes drive, determination, and a persistence that is hard to quantify. These qualities will develop further when you enter the workplace and stand face to face with the demands and challenges of a career in communications, but you have to prepare yourself now if you hope to be ready later on.

4. START A PROFESSIONAL CONTACT LIST

How do you keep track of the phone numbers and e-mail addresses of your friends and family? If you have information scribbled down on scraps of paper that are shoved into a drawer in your desk or written in the back of a datebook, the time has come to begin thinking more professionally about the people you know—your contacts. It may be difficult to believe now, but the guy or girl sitting next to you in class may be one of your best contacts for future employment at some point in your career. Class guest speakers, internship supervisors, even the barista at your favorite coffee shop are all people whose basic contact information should be kept in some organized, retrievable form, preferably in a digital form that can be duplicated in case you lose it or your computer crashes. But even an old-fashioned paper address book can do the trick.

You know that you need to input contacts' cell numbers, e-mail addresses, and social networking accounts. But you should also include information that will help you network with them more efficiently—for example, their birthdays, names of siblings, high schools and colleges, internship situations, favorite bands, personal interests, projects that you worked on together, various jobs they've held, and other information. Most people think that we (the authors) know a lot of people. But without our Mac Address Books, we'd be lost. After every meeting we attend, we jot down a few things that we learned about the person during that meeting. That way, the next time we see the person, we can say, "How was that vacation to St. Lucia you took last month?" or "How did that client presentation go?" This isn't dishonest or calculating; we honestly care about the people we meet. But there's no way that we could keep track of these details without a system. Unfortunately, we didn't start keeping our lists until years after college, and we've lost forever the names of classroom guest speakers and the people and companies that gave us informational interviews. Thankfully, you still have time.

If you have a PC with Microsoft Office, it's already loaded with Microsoft Outlook; in fact, you may already be using Outlook to manage your e-mail. But the Outlook address book is a contact list just waiting for your contacts! The same is true for Mac users and their Address Book function, smartphone users, and the Contact List function for many e-mail providers. The Internet is filled with companies offering free database or contact management software. Always remember to find out who will have access to your personal information and how it is backed up.

5. BE A HISTORY BUFF

We can't stress enough the necessity of knowing as much about history as possible. What history? All history: It's hard to eliminate any areas or periods. Consider that good decisions are made in context. All aspects of communications work—from creation to distribution— demand decision making, and decisions that bear fruit for an individual or a company are good for many reasons. Historical context is a tool that you can use to improve your decision making. The history of a community, a region, a company, an individual, a continent, or an ethnic group can be helpful. For example, how could a journalist do a good job in the Middle East if he or she did not know about previous conflicts and achievements of the people in that area? The same is true for many other fields. A Hollywood writer who submits a new quiz-show idea to a television network had better know the history of television quiz shows. Trying to accomplish communications work when you do not know the historical context will ultimately catch up with you.

Be sure to keep up with current events as well. After all, they are history in the making. If you do, you will be able to incorporate what you've learned into your classroom participation, your writing, and eventually your on-the-job responsibilities. Let's say that one day you're asked to join a team assigned to develop a marketing plan for your company. The meetings are taking place in another part of the company, and when the team meets, you discover that you know no one. However, knowing current events will help you take part in informal conversations prior to the meeting and may even contribute to the development of the marketing plan. Put in place now the activities that will help you land a good job and excel in it once you get there.

6. LEARN AS MUCH AS YOU CAN ABOUT COMPUTERS AND SOFTWARE

As you know, different computer technologies are essential in all communications and media. You should know how to do the following:

- Use several types of software programs—word processing, presentation and spreadsheet programs, video editing, and creating basic graphics.
- Use e-mail to communicate effectively with people in your daily life. You should know basic e-mail commands well enough to be able to communicate with individuals and groups, forward mail, and send attachments.
- Use the Internet for research and e-library search tools.
- Set up and edit a homepage and stream video and audio on the Internet.
- Load software and move around in applications on your company's menu of software.
- Set up a computer and presentation workstation and get the cables in the right places.
- Load and unjam the paper in a computer printer or photocopier—and be willing to do so.

Computer literacy demands many skills and is critical to success today. Many companies have special applications designed for their business or field, such as marketing databases, client-tracking systems, or project cost analyses. Some of these applications will be unavailable to learn until you're in a job or an internship. If that is the case, be sure to ask about training programs once you're in. If the company does not provide a training program, see if someone in the company will get you started. Otherwise, obtain the operating manuals, and learn what you can on your own. As a last resort, enroll in a vendor training program to learn the application. The cost of the program will be a smart investment in your future. In a larger sense, new technologies are often the reason for innovation and change in communications and media businesses. Even if you are not technically oriented, don't let yourself be afraid of technology. Embrace new technologies as much as possible. Those who can ride the new waves of technology have a much better chance for employment and higher pay.

One way to enhance your computer expertise is to select information science, management information systems, or information technology as a minor concentration during your college studies. The body of computer coursework has various names and subspecialties. If you have the interest and aptitude, it would be wise to consider a computer-related minor.

7. BECOME A RESEARCH AND JOB SEARCH EXPERT

Your college library's reference works are gold mines for information on the media/communications industries. Most fields have yearbooks, such as the *Broadcasting & Cable Yearbook* (http://www.bowker.com /index.php/component/content/article/2/33). This work starts with a preface that provides a concise description of major developments and trends in the field. The book is divided into specialties with lists of organizations for radio, TV, and cable. Also, you will find sections on government agencies and ownership; equipment suppliers and services; programming suppliers; associations, education, and awards; and books, periodicals, and videos.

Of course, the Internet is the resource of all resources when preparing for a job search. First, the Web is an amazing research tool that allows you to find information about almost anything—the industries, the organizations, and often the people with whom you need to connect. Thousands of jobs are listed on the Internet, and many job-listing sites focus on the media and communications fields. Second, you can promote yourself by putting your resumé in a virtual job bank. In fact, putting resumés and cover letters on the Internet is a common method of launching a job search. It makes it easier for people worldwide to find you.

Before you begin your job search, make a list of the specific job categories that interest you. You will not get far unless you know the names of positions such as *copy writer, video producer,* and so on. It's a learn-as-you-go process, and it is essential that you learn the proper keywords to use for searching. Most job banks will help you learn these. Some search engines will require you to enter such information as job title, location, discipline (marketing, public relations), and salary range or to search by date of posting, so be ready to follow directions carefully. You will find that some search engines are easy to use, whereas others make the task more difficult than it's worth. Some job banks list jobs for all fields (for example, monster.com), and some job banks are specific to the media and communications world (such as tvjobs.com).

However, doing an Internet job search is not as clear-cut as you would think. There are so many Web sites that a good way to find the right one(s) is to get a small group of people together, divide the addresses among them, and have each search ten addresses, taking careful notes or printing home pages with addresses and tables of contents. This record keeping is important. Many people do not keep track of their searches and have no record of the useful information they have found. Internet searches may seem time-consuming, but they are not nearly as

ON THE JOB: Recruiting Shifts

A major change I've noticed about recruiting for entry-level positions in the past few years is the lack of preparation (for the interview) by the individual. Many of the candidates we've interviewed didn't have the first inkling about our operation. With all of the information available via the Internet and our Web site—98 percent of the candidates had not even visited our Web site for information about our business.

Dan Scheidel
Public broadcasting executive

time-consuming as needlessly sending your resumé to the wrong person or to a company that doesn't really fit your interests.

Some Internet sites provide information about internships or advice on subjects such as improving job-interview skills. Others allow you to post your resumé: Just be sure to follow the directions carefully, as they can differ from site to site. When doing this, remember to save your resumé as a plain-text file. This will eliminate any bold and italic type but will help ensure that your resumé is correctly formatted when it's posted. Two sites that will help you prepare your resumé and cover letter plus provide you with a variety of worthwhile services and listings are collegerecruiter.com (http://www.collegerecruiter.com) and e-career center.com (http://www.e-careercenter.com). A site that coordinates activities with colleges is MonsterCollege (http://college.monster.com). It is a comprehensive site that has job search tips, networking ideas and opportunities, and recent hiring news. In addition, it can help you with resumés and cover letters, and it provides samples of each. Using Internet search engines to find job postings and information is also helpful and one of the most common search techniques today. Using google.com, hotjobs.com, or yahoo.com will open up many avenues for you.

Most jobs today are publicized through Internet postings. Even when actual jobs are not posted, the Internet is a primary source for job leads, which can ultimately lead to interviews. Once you get on the "short list" of those being considered for a particular job, you may be asked to answer questions via e-mail as a pre-interview technique.

In addition to the following lists of Internet job sites, you can consult any organizations that would logically list jobs—for example, professional organizations such as the National Association of Broadcasters (http://www.nab.org), industry trade publications such as *Advertising Age* (http://www.adage.com), and specific companies such as CBS (http://www.cbs.com). Professional organizations often have job services. The Radio-Television News Directors' Association and Foundation (www.rtndf.org) has a good one. NBC (http://www.nbcunicareers.com) has an "Early Career Programs" section on its Web site listing several initiatives specifically for new college graduates. One such program is the News Associates Program that hires competent college graduates for the network and moves them through several opportunities over a one-year period.

Another technique is to search by state, city, or regional Web site. This is an excellent strategy; often you know what region of the country you want to live in even if you aren't sure what kind of job you want. Listed here are twelve state Web site addresses; many of these sites have links to other regional or city job banks. You can easily find other state job banks through a Web search or a phone call to a state government office.

State Job Banks

Alabama	http://joblink.alabama.gov
Alaska	http://www.jobs.state.ak.us
California	http://www.caljobs.ca.gov
Florida	http://www.floridajobs.org/workforce/os_job _search.html
Georgia	http://www.dol.state.ga.us/js/find_a_job.htm
Iowa	http://www.iowaworkforce.org/newjobs.htm
Maryland	http://www.careernet.state.md.us
New York	http://www.labor.ny.gov/lookingforajob.shtm
Ohio	https://ohiomeansjobs.com/omj/ and http://jfs.ohio.gov/0001ourservices.stm
South Carolina	http://www.state.sc.us/jobs
Utah	http://jobs.utah.gov/
Wisconsin	http://www.dwd.state.wi.us/jobnet/mapwi.htm

The following are lists of other career-related Web sites. Searching both general sites and specific job banks can be good places to start a job search. An asterisk indicates that an organization is one of the larger job-bank sites. If these larger sites are not productive, try some of the smaller ones, such as http://www.mediarecruiter.com or http:// www.mediabistro.com.

General Job Banks

*America's Job Bank	http://www.ajb.dni.us
Best Jobs USA	http://www.bestjobsusa.com
Broadcast Employment	http://www.tvjobs.com
*CareerBuilder	http://www.careerbuilder.com
Career Magazine	http://www.careermag.com
Career Rookie	http://www.careerrookie.com
*College Grad	http://www.collegegrad.com
Craigslist	http://www.craigslist.org
*Federal Jobs	http://www.fedworld.gov/jobs/jobsearch.html
High-Tech Jobs	http://dice.com
HotJobs	http://www.hotjobs.com
JobBank USA	http://www.jobbankusa.com
JobHunt	http://www.job-hunt.org
JobTRAK	http://www.monstertrak.monster.com
Manpower	http://www.manpower.com
Marketing Jobs	http://www.marketingjobs.com
*Monster Jobs	http://www.monster.com
Monster+Hot Jobs	http://hotjobs.yahoo.com
*National Association of Broadcasters	http://www.nab.org
*National Association of Colleges and Employers	http://www.jobweb.org
National Association of Television Program Executives	http://www.careers.natpe.org
NationJob Network	http://www.nationjob.com
Writing Jobs	http://www.writejobs.com

Specific Job Banks

Advertising Sales Jobs	http://www.mediastaffingnetwork.com
Asian American Journalists Association	http://www.aaja.org/membership/career_listings
Big TV Job List	http://bigtvjoblist.com
Black Broadcasters Alliance	http://www.ibbainc.com
California Chicano News Media Association	http://www.ccnma.org
Cynopsis Media	http://www.cynopsis.com
Entertainment Careers	http://www.entertainmentcareers.net
Investigative Reporters and Editors Job Center	http://www.ire.org/jobs

I Want Media-Jobs	http://www.iwantmedia.com/jobs
Journalism Jobs	http://www.journalismjobs.com
Mandy (film and TV production jobs)	http://www.mandy.com
The Maslow Media Group	http://www.maslowmedia.com
Media Bistro Jobs	http://www.mediabistro.com
the MEDIA Job	http://www.us.themediajob.com
MediaMatch	http://www.media-match.com/usa
Newsroom Jobs	http://www.newsroomjobs.com
PR Jobs-PRWeek	http://www.prweekus.com/jobs/section/257
Reality Staff	http://www.realitystaff.com
Telecommunications Careers	http://www.telecomcareers.net
TV News Jobs	http://www.tvspy.com/jobbank.cfm
Variety: Careers	http://www.variety.com/careers
Yahoo! Careers	http://careers.yahoo.com

Other Career Resources

CareerJournal: Job Hunting Tips	http://www.careerjournal.com/jobhunting
Careers in Business	http://www.careers-in-business.com
Wall Street Journal	http://www.careers.wsj.com
What Color Is Your Parachute?	http://www.jobhuntersbible.com

8. LEARN TO SPEAK AND WRITE A FOREIGN LANGUAGE

Computer-related fields have been mentioned as possible minors. Today an argument could also be made for electing a foreign language as a minor concentration in college so that you can speak and write a second language fluently after graduation. We know of a local high-tech company that is advertising for technical writers who have good writing skills in English and Spanish to write product descriptions for its catalog. Technical writers are in demand, but bilingual technical writers face little competition. Knowing a second language can help you obtain higher salaries, better job security, and greater mobility.

Another opportunity that is offered by a second language is travel. The world becomes your potential job market. That's an exciting possibility. With the uncertainties that communications/media professionals face, developing fluency in a second language is one of the best things that you can do to enhance your career.

9. TAKE A BUSINESS COURSE

Add to your knowledge and understanding of business by enrolling in a business course while you're in college. Take the course that is offered by the business college or department, not just the one offered by the media or communications department. Taking the course through the business school will put you in a room with other business-minded students and give you a better feel for how business people approach their discipline. In a basic business course, you will learn about budgets, simple accounting procedures, business plans, projecting costs, and other areas that are important to business success. Not only will this information help you in your own professional (and personal) life, but it will project to prospective employers an understanding that the media business, for all its creativity and entertainment, is just that—a business.

10. WRITE YOUR IDEAL RESUMÉ

As early in your college career as possible, write a one-page resumé that includes your grade point average, internships, work experiences, volunteer and special activities, professional memberships, awards, and anything else you would like to learn or take part in during your college years. Dream a little. Give yourself something to work toward. For example, jotting down some specific future summer work experiences on paper will make it easier for you to focus on and achieve that goal. The same is true for any other experience or opportunity you aspire to. You will almost always achieve more when you work toward clearly defined goals.

11. WRITE A REAL RESUMÉ AND COVER LETTER, AND HAVE BOTH READY AT ALL TIMES

Starting now, you should have a resumé and cover letter ready at all times. You will be drafting and redrafting your resumé for the rest of your professional life, so you might as well start preparing now. If you're resisting this activity because you fear that you have nothing to write, face your fear and decide how you're going to deal with that reality. If you're resisting because the task of organizing your life into a one-page document is just too daunting, get help. Most of the career Web sites listed earlier provide resumé templates to help get you started. You can even download templates from Microsoft Office Word. Remember— prospective internships, prospective employers, and even professors you might ask for recommendations are going to ask to see your resumé.

Numerous books are available to help you draft an appropriate, eye-catching, honest resumé, so we won't go into detail here. Our main point is for you to write one *now*. Save multiple versions of your resumé so you can use the appropriate resumé for the appropriate job. You may feel that a paper resume is *so* last decade, but in addition to a Web site or digital portfolio, you will most certainly be asked to provide a hard copy of your resumé at some point. Be ready for that request.

Once it's written, be ready to give the resumé to someone on a moment's notice. That means updating your resumé every time something resumé-worthy happens to you, in addition to asking trusted family members, academic contacts, and even peers to review it occasionally. Don't get caught trying to draft or fix your entire resumé overnight when someone requests it.

12. KEEP A PORTFOLIO

Starting right now, set up two portfolios. Portfolios are basically folders that are designed to keep materials for later presentation or review. The first portfolio should be filled with whatever represents your talents and hard work best—all of your best papers, scripts, photographs, press kits, research projects, magazine and newspaper articles, videos, multimedia work, graphic design projects, etc. Assume that you will be asked to show some of these items to prospective employers. Organize and edit this material so that the best of your portfolio can be carried and shown easily and quickly. If you can, make at least two copies of your portfolio so that you can leave one copy with an employer if necessary. Then store it in a safe place. This first portfolio should also be available online. See Tip 13 ("Create a Personal Web Page") for more information.

The second portfolio should be filled with samples of communications that interest you. It's easy to download newspaper articles from Internet sources, saving you the trouble of cutting, pasting, and photocopying articles. Many movies, television shows, radio programs, and DVDs can also be purchased. Sponsoring organizations might give you press kits if you ask for them. Once you start keeping a file, find useful ways to categorize items for easy referral. Classroom projects, team projects, and papers can often be enhanced by what you've collected in your file.

13. CREATE A PERSONAL WEB PAGE

In addition to a paper resumé and portfolio, you need to create a central *online* presence for your work and yourself. Consider this online space

---

ON THE JOB: We See You Online

The Web and social media have completely changed the face of all facets of recruiting. It is so much easier to find and view people's work on the Web. We can get a feel for their creativity through their online reel (portfolio), but the Web site itself tells us a lot about a candidate.

Steve Cippollone
Film and video production company executive

---

as separate from your social networking page or other professional network link. It should be a site about you and you alone.

Do you own the Web address for your name (i.e., www.sherrihope culver.com)? If you don't, you should! For under $12 a year you can purchase a URL at www.GoDaddy.com. There are numerous Web site templates available free online, and it's easy set to up a basic site. Don't worry about creating an extremely technologically advanced Web presence. Your site just needs to represent you professionally and provide easy access to your resumé and portfolio materials, particularly for potential employers if you decide to include this URL on your resumé.

If your portfolio materials are already available online, consider your site as an aggregated location for all information and links about you. This is your opportunity to pull together your online brand, the brand of "You." After all, there is always information about us online that we have little control over. There should be at least one place online where your presence is managed only by you. This is that space!

14. CLEAN UP YOUR ONLINE LIFE

One of the most important steps you must take before beginning your job (or internship) search is to take a close look at the information available about you on the Internet. That means carefully reviewing social networking pages (yours and those of your friends), photo-sharing sites, and other online spaces for any inappropriate content about you. If you find any, you must delete that content or ask your friends to delete it for you. In the last few years, there has been increasing anecdotal evidence that students' postgraduate employment opportunities can be negatively influenced by inappropriate online material from their college days. Don't let this happen to you.

The first thing a potential employer is going to do is "Google" your name. Have you done this yet? If not, now's the time. Input your name, hit "Enter" and see what comes up. Be sure to check various configurations of your name if you use one version with friends and another at school or work (i.e., using "Samuel" when you're at work, but "Sam" at home).

If you're wondering what material qualifies as "inappropriate," here's an easy test. Before you upload anything to a social networking site, think about the CEO of the company you dream of working for discovering those photos . . . or your parents. If you think that discovery would be fine, it's okay to keep the content. If not, delete it. If you truly can't bear to remove anything, go through your privacy settings and ensure that no one can see your content except your friends (not "friends of friends"). After you've done your best to clean up your spaces, ask a family friend to Google you and report what they find. Be sure to ask if anything concerns them, as it would likely concern potential employers, too. Remember, online content can follow you around for years, and we're amazed at how few students (or working professionals) take the time to monitor their online presence. Clean it up now and make this an annual exercise. Your future self will thank you for it.

4

GETTING STARTED IN YOUR SEARCH

This chapter is filled with recommendations that can turn your search from just-like-everyone-else's into one that helps make you uniquely qualified for a position. From assessing your personality type to tackling team projects, these tips are critical for short- and long-term success. Don't try to put them all into action at once. Begin with just a few, and then build your skills and tactics from there.

15. LEARN THE TERMINOLOGY

Every business has its own terminology and acronyms. In many cases, this terminology is used liberally every day. It is important that you know and become comfortable using the terminology in regular conversation. Suppose that you are on the first day of a new job and someone says something like this:

"Roger, could you go to the supply room and get me a DVD-R, two zip drives, and that old one-inch tape that's in the corner?"[1] (Television commercial production)

"Jan, we're going to have to do some quick research on these trends. Do a ProQuest search to see what has been written about them." (Marketing or any field)

---

[1] *DVD-R* refers to a recordable digital video disc or digital versatile disc; one-inch is a videotape format.

"Carol, your first assignment will be writing three PSAs[2] for Quality Corp. Here's some background to read before you go home tonight." (Public relations)

Assuming that one of the preceding scenarios is related to your specialty, would you know what was being asked of you? If you are not familiar with the terminology used, look in the back of any textbook that covers basic communications industries for a glossary of terminology. A glossary could easily include hundreds of terms. You should learn the terminology well enough to use the terms comfortably in business conversation.

16. TEAM PROJECTS YIELD TEAM PLAYERS

We don't know anyone who accomplishes communications work entirely alone. Perhaps a few Web site operators or someone writing a small newsletter does so. Even famous novelists work with publishing companies that employ people who edit, market, and sell their books. Indeed, teamwork is an accepted and essential way of accomplishing work. Since you will succeed or fail by the quality of the work that emanates from your team, you must be able to be a team player, which means (1) playing many different roles, (2) solving problems on the spot, and (3) being assigned a task, working separately to accomplish it, and bringing it back to the team for evaluation and correction.

Diversity is a key characteristic of many successful teams. When you're on a team, particularly for the first time, look around to see what unique skills each person brings to the team. Then ask yourself, "What do I bring?" Consider your strengths, but don't overextend yourself.

Male, female, African American, Latino, young, old, creative, technical, experienced, new-to-the-job: these terms express the diversity that you are likely to find on a team. Diverse perspectives expand the range of ideas considered and act as checks and balances in sifting out less-effective approaches. The following is a list of ideas and actions to practice when working in groups.

- **Listening/observing/thinking/brainstorming.** These highly focused and energy-consuming activities are the foundation of good teamwork. Without them you can't fully understand the mission of the team or the expected work flow. Make sure that you understand the parameters of any brainstorming session you attend. Are you working

---

[2] *PSA* refers to a public service announcement.

in a judgment-free environment in which all ideas are welcome? How are the ideas evaluated and organized during the session?

- **Making contributions.** Active participation is essential. Sitting there like a bump on a log will not do. Contributions mean preparation. If that means burning the midnight oil or arriving an hour before everyone else, do it. Newcomers should contribute carefully at first and only after the seasoned veterans have set the pace. Look for areas where you can offer to do extra work or solve a problem. This is one way to establish a solid, hardworking reputation while also helping drive a project to completion.

- **Controlling emotions.** Exuberance is desirable, but anger, bitterness, or criticism of others in a group situation can be very damaging. Making negative comments about fellow employees is off-limits in person, on the phone, and online. Negative remarks made on social networking sites, through e-mail, or via text messages can easily be saved, shared, and forwarded to coworkers. Such behavior may also make you a target of criticism. If you can be a positive force, you will be recognized as an outstanding contributor and a valuable employee worthy of others' trust and further responsibility in the workplace.

- **Problem solving.** Find a way to solve problems that are appropriate for you. If that means delivering things, researching, coordinating schedules, or assisting in the preparation of presentations, offer to do those tasks. By doing such things, you're showing that you understand the pressure of deadlines and the need for productivity.

- **Be willing to compromise.** Learn the art of compromise. It's not easy, but it's essential if a team is to be productive.

17. PROMOTE YOURSELF WITHOUT BEING OBNOXIOUS

Professors, bosses, or other important people don't know what your competencies and life goals are (and sometimes forget them, even if you have told them). If you are working on a class project, for example, it's to your benefit to keep track of your contributions, the hours that you've spent, and the lessons you have learned. Although you hope it won't happen, while working on a group project you may need these records to support or defend your work. Or you may need to explain to a professor why you have spent ten extra hours on the project. This could be considered either self-promotion or just information that an evaluator needs to know when reviewing your performance. If done correctly and not too frequently, it will help you.

The same applies in the workplace: Making sure that your efforts are known is important. You can do this verbally, with a written memo, or by e-mail. Written records are especially important, since they can be used during a performance evaluation, which most organizations conduct annually.

18. JOIN A PROFESSIONAL ORGANIZATION

Professional organizations exist for many reasons—to promote a specialization (such as photography, marketing, or video games) and to provide services (such as conferences, seminars, awards ceremonies, and networking). Many organizations publish directories, newsletters, and magazines. They hold annual meetings and assist local chapters, which usually meet monthly. All communications and media industries have at least one professional organization, and these groups are extremely valuable for both new and seasoned members. Many organizations have college chapters that are inexpensive to join and are advised by a professor. By the time you are a junior in college, it is advisable to be a member of at least the college chapter, to attend the monthly meetings, and to take part in any activities the group sponsors. Often, college chapters invite professionals from the community to speak at their meetings. These presentations are a wonderful networking opportunity and a perfect time to learn more about the professional activities in your community.

Make it a goal to introduce yourself to these speakers, to make an impression on them, to see if you can get an invitation to visit their business, or obtain a business card. Even better, if you know of a research group or similar resource on campus that might help this speaker in his or her business, don't hesitate to tell the speaker about it, and follow up if you can. Being helpful to someone makes it likely that you will be remembered.

The monthly meetings of many local off-campus professional chapters are held at a different business location each month. You can learn a lot by attending these meetings and seeing businesses firsthand. Employees of the business host the meeting, so you are often given personal tours in which the business activities are explained, and you are given the chance to meet a variety of employees and view the facilities. We have found that many businesses are larger and more diversified than we had originally thought. An added benefit of attending these meetings is that you will find yourself inside businesses that you might otherwise have a difficult time entering. By attending a professional organizational meeting, you are going as an honored guest; you may learn things that you would not otherwise be told because you are part of a gathering of like-minded professionals. Not all professional chapters allow college-student members to attend meetings on a regular basis, but you should inquire.

While attending a meeting, you will be rubbing shoulders with professionals from various parts of your community and from different sections of the business. It would take weeks, even months, to meet all these people—even if you had the time to do so. So when you get to attend a meeting such as this, treat it as a chance of a lifetime. Afterward, make notes on the people you met. Add names to your Professional Contact List (see Tip 4). Write down in your notebook any interesting points you learned that will help you reestablish a relationship with these people later when you are job hunting. If anyone at the meeting gives you advice or is especially helpful, write a thank-you note immediately. Remember that one of the most important actions you can take to prepare yourself for life after college is to develop relationships with key people.

If you can't find a local professional organization in your specialty or if you want more information about any of the organizations discussed here, visit the Web site for the *Encyclopedia of Associations* (http://library .dialog.com/bluesheets/html/bl0114.html). This reference site lists organizations under categories such as advertising, broadcasting, and so on. You should also conduct a deeper Internet search by typing in the name of the organization as your keyword. Finally, it is worthwhile to call the organization and ask about its activities, membership dues, and publications. If you find that the organization doesn't seem appropriate for you, ask what other groups might be better suited to your specialty. Table 4.1 includes some important professional organizations (with their Web sites and phone numbers). Many of these associations also have Facebook pages and post frequently to Twitter.

19. VOLUNTEER

Provide communications services on a volunteer basis for small or campus-related organizations. For example, write press releases for your sorority or soccer team. Help out a TV station sponsoring a 10k run by offering to deliver materials, doing behind-the-scenes work, or whatever else is necessary. If it's not directly communications work, that's okay. Volunteering will often bring you unexpected rewards, such as opportunities to meet professionals who might hire you someday.

The Hands On Network (http://www.handsonnetwork.org) can introduce you to local volunteer opportunities in your community. If you live in a major metropolitan area, you might also find a local affiliation

Table 4.1 Professional Organizations

Organization	Web Site	Telephone
Academy of Motion Picture Arts and Sciences	www.oscars.org	310-247-3000
Academy of Television Arts and Sciences (ATAS)	www.emmys.com	818-754-2800
Advertising Club of New York	www.theadvertisingclub.org	212-533-8080
Advertising Production Club (APC) of New York	www.apc-ny.org	212-671-2975
Alliance for Women in Media (AWM)	www.allwomeninmedia.org	703-506-3290
American Advertising Federation (AAF)	www.aaf.org	202-898-0089
American Institute of Graphic Arts (AIGA)	www.aiga.com	212-807-1990
American Marketing Association (AMA)	www.marketingpower.com	312-542-9000 or 800-AMA-1150
American News Women's Club (ANWC)	www.anwc.org	202-332-6770
American Society of Journalists and Authors (ASJA)	www.asja.org	212-997-0947
American Society of Magazine Editors (ASME)	www.magazine.org/asme	212-872-3700
American Society of Newspaper Editors (ASNE)	www.asne.org	703-453-1122
American Sportscasters Association (ASA)	www.americansportscastersonline.com	212-227-8080
Asian American Journalists Association (AAJA)	www.aaja.org	415-346-2051
Association of Graphic Communications (AGC)	www.agcomm.org	212-279-2100
Cable and Telecommunications Association for Marketing (CTAM)	www.ctam.com	703-549-4200

Table 4.1 (*continued*)

Organization	Web Site	Telephone
Creative Musicians Coalition (CMC)	www.creativemusicianscoalition.com	309-685-4843
Direct Marketing Association (DMA)	www.the-dma.org	212-768-7277
Entertainment Merchants Association (EMA)	www.entmerch.org	818-385-1500
Graphic Artists Guild (GAG)	www.gag.org	212-791-3400
Hollywood Radio and Television Society (HRTS)	www.hrts.org	818-789-1182
Independent Book Publishers Association (IBPA)	www.ibpa-online.org	310-372-2732
Independent Film and Television Alliance (IFTA)	www.ifta-online.org	310-446-1000
International Advertising Association (IAA)	www.iaaglobal.org	212-557-1133
International Animated Film Society (ASIFA Hollywood)	www.asifa-hollywood.org	818-842-8330
International Association of Business Communicators (IABC)	www.iabc.com	415-544-4700
International Documentary Association (IDA)	www.documentary.org	213-534-3600
International Food, Wine and Travel Writers Association (IFWTWA)	www.ifwtwa.org	877-439-8929
International Radio and Television Society Foundation (IRTS)	www.irts.org	212-867-6650
International Women's Writing Guild (IWWG)	www.iwwg.org	212-737-7536

Organization	Web Site	Telephone
Magazine Publishers of America	www.magazine.org	212-872-3700
National Academy of Television Arts and Sciences	www.emmyonline.org	212-586-8424
National Association of Broadcasters (NAB)	www.nab.org	202-429-5300
National Association of Television Program Executives (NATPE)	www.natpe.org	310-453-4440
Printing Industries of America	www.printing.org	800-910-4283
Public Relations Society of America (PRSA)	www.prsa.org	212-460-1400
Radio Advertising Bureau (RAB)	www.rab.com	800-232-3131
Radio Television Digital News Association (RTDNA)	www.rtdna.org	202-659-6510
Retail Advertising and Marketing Association (RAMA)	www.rama-nrf.org	202-661-3052
Romance Writers of America (RWA)	www.rwanational.org	832-717-5200
Society of Publication Designers (SPD)	www.spd.org	212-223-3332
Specialty Graphic Imaging Association (SGIA)	www.sgia.org	703-385-1335 or 888-385-3588
Women in Cable Telecommunications (WICT)	www.wict.org	703-234-9810
Women in Film (WIF)	www.wif.org	310-657-5144

of the Cares volunteer program, such as New York Cares, Boston Cares, and St. Louis Cares. After an orientation session, Cares volunteers receive monthly calendars of weekly, monthly, or one-time volunteer opportunities in their city. Also, check out Idealist.com, a national database of nonprofit organizations and volunteer opportunities.

20. CONDUCT A PERSONALITY ASSESSMENT AND DEVELOP YOUR SKILL SET

Take a critical look at yourself and your goals. What strengths do you have that will help you accomplish those goals? What are your main weaknesses that will prevent you from succeeding? What are your biases, preferences, and attitudes about others? We suggest that you begin to think about how you can build on your strengths and strengthen your weakest areas. There are many assessment tools that can help you take a deep personal inventory, ranging from formal testing (like the Myers Briggs Type Indicator or the Strong Interest Inventory) to the large sections of bookstores devoted to this topic (a best-seller since 1975 is the book *What Color Is Your Parachute?*). Assess your interpersonal and social skills as well as your technical, creative, and writing skills. These insights are not necessarily for your resumé or an interview, but they may come up. Being able to articulate your strengths and weaknesses is one of the most common interview questions.

Once you gain a deeper understanding of your strengths and weaknesses, consider selecting electives in your college coursework or seeking opportunities outside college that will help you build skills in areas where you need help. Talk to your department chair, professors, graduate assistants, fellow students, or college career officer about those interests.

For example, you may want to improve your ability to work with certain computer programs. If coursework isn't appropriate, find special short-term classes that may be listed at computer stores or advertised in a local paper, a local Web site, or a business newsweekly. They could even be offered by tutors at the campus computer lab. You may be amazed at how a little informal tutoring can advance your skills. You just need to have a questioning mind and be persistent in seeking out these kinds of opportunities.

Another possibility is to take short courses over a break or summer vacation. Devote one week to learning something new. For example, professional organizations hold workshops in team building or public speaking. There may be something offered in a one-day session or in just a few hours. These sessions might open new areas of interest for you. Look at industry Web sites and magazines for upcoming conferences, meetings, and workshops. In most fields, such events are held year-round in various locations. You may have to travel and you may have to pay, but if the experience will teach a specific skill that you feel you need to have, it will be worth it. (Look for special student rates that some of these conferences offer.)

21. ATTEND CAREER WORKSHOPS AND FAIRS

Career workshops and career fairs are plentiful. Recruiters use them as a preferred method for identifying prospective employees because they can meet candidates face-to-face and conduct brief interviews. In many cases, workshops and fairs are held at the same time and location so that you can take advantage of both. Workshops cover topics such as preparing resumés and developing interview skills. Fairs attract employers who set up kiosks where company representatives can tell you about the types of jobs available. Career fairs may be general in focus (covering many different industries) or specialized. We've seen creative-career fairs, business-related fairs, and computer/information-systems-related fairs. Cities sponsor career fairs, as do most colleges and community colleges.

Career fairs are extremely worthwhile to attend. You should start doing so long before you look for a real job. This is a terrific way for a college student to learn about the enormous number of companies doing business and the types of jobs they offer—the variety can be mind-boggling. Career fairs are concentrated experiences where you can spend an hour and receive a lifetime of benefits. All you have to do is walk around and begin talking with people. If you're close to graduation, you can have one kind of conversation with a representative; if graduation is a few years off, you can have another kind. Let's say that you're a sophomore and not sure of what you want to do after college. You could focus on general information—who is at the fair, what companies look interesting, and so on. Or you could strike up a few conversations and begin to learn what a certain company is like and what types of positions it offers. You might learn a specific fact that's really useful—for example, that a company is opening a new division next year in Florida and will be hiring about two hundred employees. You might also learn that a corporation seems very formal and therefore doesn't interest you. Even though a career fair may not be focused on internships or summer work, there's nothing stopping you from asking for and getting a contact to call. It's great when you can write or call someone and say,

"So-and-so suggested I talk with you." Your chances of connecting with someone are much greater when you are referred.

If you run out of questions, ask about the types of people the company has hired recently and the kind of background and life experiences the company is looking for in its employees. Ask also about the company's locations, benefits, and so on. Your questioning is like an open book: Just have a curious mind and a few questions ready, and the rest will happen by itself. Look for news of upcoming career fairs on trade associations' Web sites, college newspapers, city business newsweeklies, or local newspapers. Fairs are usually well advertised. If your college isn't having a career fair, check with other colleges nearby. You could also call the mayor's office or Chamber of Commerce about fairs that are being sponsored by the city government.

When you attend a career fair, it's important that you dress appropriately. Wear the same type of clothing that you would wear to a job interview—that is, fairly conservative business attire. Bring copies of your resumé, just in case, and always carry a business card containing your name, e-mail address, phone number, and industry or field of interest.

22. SURF THE NET (AND BOOKSTORES) FOR INSPIRATION

When you're researching a potential internship or the job market, you need the most current resources available. Bookstores are one place to find such texts. Begin stopping in bookstores on your way to somewhere else, but allow extra time if you can. You may find that you're staying longer than planned because the store has an excellent career section, or because you are finding so many references that interest you. Another advantage of bookstores is that many have great coffee bars. Normally, you can take books into these areas and leisurely browse through them before you buy. Don't forget to browse the magazine and newspaper sections, where you will likely find a wide selection of publications, including some that you may not be aware of. Many bookstores also provide an excellent selection of multimedia titles, music areas, and even Internet access. They've become wonderful resource/meeting/chatting places.

Searching online bookstores can turn up even more helpful, unusual, or hard-to-find books. Many Web sites (such as amazon.com and others) make recommendations for books on similar topics once you've searched for a few titles. It's easy to search for books by topic, by field or industry, by author, or by keyword. Many college and university libraries provide access to a large number of books through their online library system. If you haven't already availed yourself of this perk, check with your college librarian for guidance.

23. SEEK AN INTERNSHIP . . . OR TWO OR THREE

It's hard to find a textbook, a career guide, or even a pamphlet that doesn't recommend internships to students. That's because internships provide low-risk experiences. Everyone at the company knows that you're there to learn, so you can participate in many different activities as an assistant—an ideal learning situation. Because internships are important, they require special planning on your part.

First, an internship will be valuable only if the organization is willing to provide you with a rounded experience. Large companies with established internship programs are usually adept at providing worthwhile activities. Small companies often offer productive internship opportunities precisely because they have small staffs and few resources and are likely in need of help. Some companies have strong unions that can limit the hands-on work opportunities for interns. Be sure to ask about this, especially if you're seeking an internship at a television station or other technical or creative environment. In some cases, interns get to produce real communications, sit in on real meetings, and have the opportunity to make decisions. In other cases, however, interns are given meaningless tasks or sit at a desk surfing the Internet for a good portion of each day. An internship looks good on a resumé, but you want more than that. You want and need an experience that will help you learn specific skills and allow you to observe a wide range of activities. Even better, internships can lead to jobs. What better way for a company to get to know a potential employee than by having him or her as an intern in the office for three months? Internships provide a firsthand learning experience for students, one that cannot come from a textbook.

Finding a good internship is like looking for an apartment. You don't know much until you start to compare one opportunity with another. Once you investigate several internships, you'll be able to add up the advantages and disadvantages of each. College placement officers or student advisers can explain the internship process at your institution. Generally, companies are listed with the college placement office, which matches interns to the companies. But many internships are not advertised. Talk with your adviser or professors in your major about your interests. Some professors may have recently changed careers, coming from a communications business to a university to teach; others consult or provide part-time communications work; many attend professional meetings. These professors know which businesses in your community provide internships and may be able to put you in touch with key people.

If you connect with a company that is interested in providing an internship but is not registered with your college, you may be able to ensure that the organization does get properly listed by coordinating and following up on the process. This is good experience in itself. Though time-consuming, the effort is worthwhile because an internship can be one of your most valuable and productive college experiences. And there's no pressure because you are not asking for a job.

An excellent way to assess the value of particular internships is to talk with students presently working as interns or, better yet, to visit them at work. Find out the good, the bad, and the ugly. Nothing beats firsthand experience. You might learn things about parking (perhaps you'll have to pay $10 or more a day) and office conditions. You'll be able to make better judgments about the work, whether you'll be comfortable with the people there, and whether you think they'd be comfortable with you. The comfort factor is a critical ingredient for an internship. If you're not comfortable in the situation for any reason, or if you sense that the employer is not comfortable with you, the internship is probably not going to work well for you. In fact, it could turn into a negative situation.

If you can't visit the place of business, ask an intern to tell you about the kind of work that he or she performs there. Finally, if you don't know anyone at a particular business, make a phone call, and see if you can schedule a time to visit. Don't accept an internship sight unseen. Just like apartment hunting, you don't have to take the first one you see. It's best to find three or four internship possibilities. Investigate each one, make visits, and then decide. Good internships are competitive. You may not get the one you most want—which is a good reason to have backups. In addition, remember that everyone working in a communications business is extremely busy. Make sure that you find out all you can ahead of time so that you don't take valuable time from someone's schedule.

How far in advance should you start working on finding an internship? That depends on many factors—whether you know what you want to do, whether you have the prerequisites completed, and so on. But a good rule of thumb is the earlier, the better. If you're planning to get involved in an internship during your junior year, you should start investigating the possibilities in the fall of your sophomore year.

Many students are interested in particular internships in distant locations. Communications students at universities across the country often seek internships at the major film and television studios on the East and

West Coasts. Several media companies have studio locations in Florida as well, including Universal Studios and Disney. One student at Robert Morris University spent a summer at Universal Studios in Florida. This took a great deal of coordination with her parents and with Universal. She applied one semester prior to her internship (which wasn't ideal timing), met the application deadlines, filed the appropriate forms (including required letters of recommendation), and made a special trip for an interview. While there, she looked into housing arrangements. At first, she didn't think she would be accepted into the program, and once accepted, she was hesitant to take it because of the distance and the money involved. Finally, she did decide to spend a summer at Universal, and it turned out to be a highlight of her college career.

If you have a favorite magazine, television program, newspaper, or film company, it's likely that the company has an internship program. Long-distance internships take more research and more work to learn about and apply to, and they're often very competitive. If they appeal to you, start planning; it can be done. A high-profile or unique internship can give a competitive edge to your resumé. It shows that you think seriously about your career and that you're willing to take risks and invest extra time and effort in your preparation. It also provides excellent conversation for a job interview.

Your best bet for internship information is your own college or university career center. The information is local and time-tested. Companies that provide the better internships continue a relationship with your institution; those that don't are eliminated. Although mentioned earlier, it is worth repeating that many schools have their internships and job opportunities listed on MonsterCollege (college.monster.com). This service is easy to use, current, and has plentiful opportunities for internships. While there are many books on internships (which your college library or career office may have), for the most part they don't deliver all that they promise. *Internships* (published by Peterson's) and *The Internship Bible* (part of a Princeton Review Series) do provide general information about which companies offer opportunities, good contact information, and plenty of tips. But a book is not going to offer you the most current data on which internships are available. If you want to pursue an internship at a specific company, go to that company's Web site and see if any internship information is posted. In addition to MonsterCollege, there are many other internship sites on the Web. One is Rising Star Internships (http://www.rsinternships.com). Another approach is to use Yahoo! or Google and search under the keyword "internships." You will find many sites, such as internships.com, internweb.com, and internjobs.com. Visit a variety of these sites and compare their resources and services to determine whether a particular site will be most helpful for your needs. Some even have particular specialties. For example, The Washington Center for Internships and Academic Seminars (http://www.twc.edu) offers competitive opportunities in the Washington, D.C., area.

24. GET A PART-TIME JOB IN YOUR FIELD

If an internship can provide you with useful on-the-job experience, just think what a carefully selected summer job in your field can do. Many internships are unpaid, so a summer job in your field can really pay off—in more ways than one.

Since many students don't declare a major until their sophomore year, you really have only two summers to explore jobs related to your field of study—the summer between your sophomore and junior years and the one between your junior and senior years. To make these two summers pay off, start planning during your first year in college.

Many students stay with the kind of job they had in high school—counter person at a fast-food restaurant, lifeguard at a pool, server at a restaurant, and so on. That's okay if you think that a job is going to fall in your lap after graduation, but by now you know better. Again, attitude and motivation are the key factors. It's going to take an investigative, hard-charging approach to find something that can help you develop a career rather than just earn money for the summer.

Some people live in large cities where there are plenty of opportunities. If you do, use that to your advantage. But if you live in a small town or rural area where there are fewer opportunities, you will have to be more resourceful to find something worthwhile. If you can't find something suitable, consider living for a summer with a relative or friend in a city where opportunities abound. These ideas may take considerable effort. The planning will demand sacrifices, but you have to keep asking yourself how important that job after college is to you. The more you prepare, the better off you'll be.

25. GET OVER YOUR FEAR OF THE COLD CALL

Often, the difference between the student who gets the great internship and the one who doesn't is the willingness of the student to pick up the phone and talk to a complete stranger. Effective "cold calling" is one of the most important social skills you should develop. Elements of cold calling include many of the same elements as general phone etiquette—speaking clearly, having a phone voice that conveys professionalism, and having a sensitivity to the subtleties of the voice of the person you're calling that can alert you to a lack of time or other problems. Life is full of occasions when a well-placed phone call (not an e-mail) can yield a unique opportunity, and the chance of an internship or a potential job is one of them. Don't let your fear of reaching a rude secretary or an annoyed employee stop you from making the call. Simply learn the skills of effective cold calling. And learn how to end a phone call with the door open, regardless of the attitude of the person on the other end of the line. Remember, "no" really just means "not now."

If you hear of a communications business or project that sounds interesting, try to find a way to visit and see what's going on. Make a cold call, and explain your interest: "Would it be possible to visit?" Often the answer will be yes. If the answer is no, try different businesses. Many students are afraid to make cold calls, but you should realize that students have a special status. In a sense, your status is neutral; you're not threatening because you are not yet looking for a job and you are expressing a desire to learn. Most professionals, even the busy ones, will try to help a student because the professional can remember being in the same position. If one professional can't help you, ask whether he or she can recommend someone else who could. Remember, when you make a cold call, your job is to establish a relationship with the first person you talk to so that, if necessary, you can be referred to someone else who can help you. Businesses are very specialized, and large businesses may have a communications department whose job it is to assist people like you. Even in small businesses, you may have to go through several referrals to find someone helpful. But make that your goal: Find someone who can help you. Don't expect it to be the first person on the other end of the line.

In addition, when making cold calls to organizations, be prepared to navigate the voice-mail system. In some cases, that may mean staying on the line or dialing zero. If cold calling does not work out for you, try e-mailing the organization. Once you know one e-mail address, you can often figure out others, and many people, even top-level executives, will respond to you faster by e-mail than by phone. The main thing to remember is that communicating with professionals as a student is likely to yield positive results. Another possibility is to go on class-sponsored field trips or tag along (with permission, of course) with a different class on its field trip. Set a goal to make a couple of visits during the school year and at least one over the summer. Take along your resumé. We have seen job offers made to students who have left their resumés at companies during field visits.

26. SET UP INFORMATIONAL INTERVIEWS

Let's say that you're considering working in the publishing industry after you graduate. You're majoring in nonfiction writing. You're doing well in your coursework, and you enjoy your courses and professors. But you don't know much about the publishing industry. What is it actually like? What do people do every day? Would you like the people who work in this industry, and would you fit in? What types of jobs are there? What are salaries like, and is there a good career path? Where would you likely be five to ten years down the road? Even if you have had an internship in the field, you still may not know the answers to many of these questions.

Talking with a professor or to a counselor in the career office is helpful. Both, however, are likely to bring up the idea of the informational interview. Informational interviews are merely exploratory meetings with people working in your field of interest. Who knows better what's going on in a field and what it is really like than those who work in it every day? If you are able to sit down and talk with some of these people, you could learn a lot. You could meet people who might hire you or who could tell you about other interesting opportunities. They may also refer you to others who might be hiring.

Informational interviews will help you in finding a job even though they are not job interviews. This is an extremely important point. You are seeking information, not employment. As soon as you say, "Do you have any job openings?" the door closes. The fact is, you are seeking information, and there is much you need to know. There is nothing dishonest about it, and you do not need to worry that the interviewer will see through your motivation. You are asking people to talk about themselves and their work, and this is usually an easy sell. People like doing this. The information they provide and the contacts you acquire will help you find that all-important job. The following steps outline how to find, arrange, and conduct informational interviews.

1. *Whom do you know in your field of interest?* Probably more people than you think. Friends, family, relatives of your classmates, colleagues where you work or used to work, neighbors, and so on may all have unexpected connections to an industry in which you're interested. People you meet on an airplane, at a college event, or at a conference are all possibilities, too. Actually, chance encounters can work in your favor and are more common than most people think. You just have to be open and recognize the possibilities when you are traveling or attending an event, such

as a luncheon for the radio and TV club or the local chapter of a professional organization.

Social networking sites can also be incredibly useful in this area. Friends of friends of friends are just a click away. If you want to meet a person from a particular business, post a request on your social networks and you'll be amazed at the links you'll discover.

If you mostly use social networking sites to connect with friends and family, consider joining a professional social networking site, such as www.linkedin.com. On Linkedin, you can create a profile that focuses on your professional experience and goals, as well as your interests and volunteer activities. There's even a space for recommendations where past employers or teachers can post a few sentences about why you're a great worker or share information about your talents in ways that you just can't write about yourself. Your links will begin to accumulate in the same way they do with other social networking sites, only these contacts will be focused on your professional career. Of course, that means the content you post should be focused exclusively on your professional activities. (For more information on creating a professional online presence, see Tip 13, "Create a Personal Web Page.")

2. *Begin to set up the interviews.* Once you have a list of people to contact, start with those you know or to whom you can be referred. A personal introduction, phone call, or e-mail on your behalf is best, but the hardest to achieve. If you are offered an introduction, you may be asked what you would like to have emphasized in this introduction. For example, you've been interested in writing since you were a child, you've had part-time jobs in the field, and so on. Think ahead of time about which of your strengths you would like to have included in an introduction.

It's likely that you will be setting up interviews with strangers, and this may sound intimidating to some. (See Tip 25, "Get Over Your Fear of the Cold Call," above.) It's not as bad as you think because most people are receptive to an informational interview. It's not about a job; it's about learning. It's not hard for your host because he or she already knows the information that will be discussed. People are busy, yes, and this will be your biggest hurdle, but all you need is about twenty minutes. Without an introduction, you could make your pitch by writing a letter, sending an e-mail, posting a message through a social or professional networking site, or calling to set up the interview. It's really your choice. The letter is the most time-consuming but perhaps the least intimidating.

Your career office may have examples of typical letters asking for informational interviews. This method may be the most appropriate if you are calling on someone older (over age fifty-five) or high in the ranks of a company. Don't eliminate higher-ups if you have the confidence to do it, but interviews with lower-level managers can be equally informative. No matter which way you decide to go, you'll need to prepare a thirty-second purpose statement. It should state who you are, what you are studying, and that you want to learn more about the realities and opportunities in that field. It's that simple: You want to learn more.

3. *Prepare for the interview by learning about the company.* The company Web site is a good place to start. If you have trouble, ask a research librarian to help you find other resources. Find a mission statement if you can, and look for information about the company's major business areas and recent successes. Prepare questions; general ones are fine, and honest ones are even better. Some typical questions are listed here:
   - What do you like best about your job?
   - What excites you most about your job?
   - What are some of the more difficult parts of the job?
   - How did you choose this field?
   - Do you work alone or in teams?
   - How is this field developing and changing?
   - What are the most important skills to have for success in this field?
   - Is a master's degree required for advancement in this field?
   - What is a typical entry-level salary in this field?
   - What is a typical career path for someone in this field?
   - Now that you know a little about me, what advice do you have for me as I think about entering this field?
   - Would you have time to critique my resumé? How could I improve it?
   - Can you recommend friends or colleagues with whom you think it would be good for me to talk?

   You don't want to seem like a know-it-all, but you do want to appear knowledgeable, curious, intelligent, and hardworking. The interviewer should see you as someone who is willing to learn and contribute to a company. Be prepared to deliver the brief statement you have developed about yourself. Practice it aloud. (This is your "elevator speech" from Tip 37, "Learn to Network.") You're likely to be asked this first. Being well-read and knowing current events is also important. It demonstrates that you have a seriousness of purpose and that you have applied yourself well during your college days. You should have copies of your resumé prepared, but do not offer one unless asked.

4. *On the day of the interview, dress professionally.* Arrive early, address your host by *Mr., Ms.,* or *Dr.,* and thank him or her sincerely for taking the time to meet with you. Avoid slang, but carry on a somewhat informal conversation. Once the interview is under way, it may turn out to be quite enjoyable because the interviewer may warm to the idea of filling you in on the real complexities and opportunities in the field. If your host recognizes you as a possible contributor in the field, you will get plenty of information, stories, and even a tour of the facilities. Don't forget to ask for additional references and a business card before you leave.

5. *Following the interview, send a formal and timely thank-you letter.* E-mail is not appropriate. After you have one interview under your belt, keep going, and try to do five or ten. They usually pay off.

27. USE CLASS ASSIGNMENTS AS OPPORTUNITIES TO MEET LEADERS IN YOUR FIELD

Starting now and continuing throughout your college years, you will be assigned projects or papers that allow you to select the topic. Use those opportunities to write about the place you'd like to work. If you're not sure where you'd like to work, use the opportunity to gain information about a place where you think you'd like to work. This is a great way to make your class assignments work for you!

Most people who have the ability to hire you have sat exactly where you're sitting now—in college, trying to figure out what to do with their lives. And because of that, you'll find that many are sympathetic to the student who wants to interview them for a research paper or project. Start by finding out what you can about the person and the company. Do an online search. Check the press section of the company Web site. Visit their Facebook or Twitter page, if they have one. Investigate a little. Prepare your questions in writing, then send an e-mail or make the call. We recommend doing the advance planning in writing because the person might respond immediately and be available to talk, and you should be prepared to answer immediately.

If you don't reach the person on your first try and need to leave a message (whether via e-mail, through a secretary, or on voice mail), begin

---

ON THE JOB: Make It Personal

Know about the BRAND of the company you're applying to. I've had people who position their whole interview around initiatives we don't do any more, or things that would never fly on the network today. It proves you don't see the big picture.

Kent Rees
Marketing executive, cable network

---

by stating, "I'm not looking for a job." Yes, you should state that clearly and directly. Provide one simple sentence explaining your request: "I'm presently enrolled in a class on (title of class). I'd like to write about (topic) for an assignment." Specify that your questions will take no more than fifteen minutes. Provide a deadline date that's at least a week away: "My project is due by (date). Perhaps we could set up a time to talk next week?" Provide your contact information. And end the message. That's all this person needs to know to decide whether to speak with you. If you think there is additional critical information that must be shared, keep it to one additional sentence. The message should be brief and to the point.

Be prepared for a reply in which the person offers to help via e-mail and asks you to send the questions. Try one more time for a phone or in-person conversation, but if e-mail is all the person offers, take it. Then add this person to your professional contact list (see Tip 4, "Start a Professional Contact List"). Finally, send a thank-you note after the conversation. If all correspondence has been via e-mail, then an e-mail thank-you is okay. But a handwritten note on professional stationery is always best.

28. LEARN ABOUT THE COMPANY BEFORE YOU ASK FOR THE JOB

Both authors of this book have interviewed and hired many people over the past twenty years, and fewer than a dozen knew anything about the companies they were applying to. Letters and interviews include oodles of information on the candidate—you. But including information about the company where you want to work will set you apart instantly. This information should not be gushing kudos about a show that you love or a video game that you can't stop playing. It should reflect a business perspective, relating to the area of work that most interests you. If you are interested in a career in producing, you might comment on the location used in a particular program, the casting, or a secondary character. If you are interested in public relations, you might comment on a recent article that mentioned one of the firm's clients.

This cannot work if you're sending a mass mailing of the same resumé and cover letter to a long list of media companies. And that's why a cover letter rarely includes such company-specific information. But if you want a job at a particular company, this action is well worth your time. It shows initiative. It shows business sense. And it will help get you noticed.

5

SUCCEEDING ONCE YOU'RE IN (YOUR INTERNSHIP OR FIRST JOB)

Congratulations! If you've landed an internship or a job, you deserve a pat on the back, a high five, or a night on the town. But your career development doesn't stop once you've landed the internship or the job; in fact, in some ways, it's just beginning. The key is using this opportunity as a stepping-stone toward your dream job (which this one probably isn't—yet). Consider these tips as ways to maximize the opportunities that lie behind every meeting, project, or assignment.

29. READ WHAT THE PROS READ

The textbooks and related readings assigned for coursework are vital to your college success and early career guidance. Read and absorb those with a passion. In addition, we're suggesting something a little different: Begin to read what communications and media professionals read to keep up on current events and developments in their industries. Industry surveys of communications executives have found that managers stay abreast of key developments in their industries through three methods:

• reading industry publications,
• attending industry conferences and seminars, and
• networking—that is, meeting and interacting with others.

Reading, attending conferences, and networking all help managers gather information, evaluate it, and (one hopes) make better decisions—from what equipment to buy, whom to hire, whom to align themselves with, what new products or services to launch, how to satisfy customers better, how much risk to take, whether to borrow money, and so on. All these decisions must be based on solid information. Fortunes and careers depend on effective decision making. Reading is one way to decrease risk and increase the chances of success.

Once you start reading, it won't be long before you realize how valuable the information can be. Almost any publication will have a few articles pertinent to your field of study or interests. As you read over a period of just one week, you will begin seeing connections among topics, and you'll be able to follow significant mergers or new product launches. As you read over a longer period of time, you will start recognizing the people, trends, and organizations that are mentioned often. Weaving this information into a conversation with a colleague or boss shows that your interest in the field extends beyond just the work you're required to do each day.

Clearly, you're not going to be able to read every publication or visit every Web site. Most people don't have the time or need for that. Instead, you should skim publications and Web sites and focus only on specific articles of interest. If you did this with two or three papers, publications, or Web sites, as some highly motivated individuals do, you would become extremely well-informed on current media activities. Over time, you would begin to see the trends that become the basis for decision making. This insight alone could give you an edge in a job interview or a chance to be noticed in your first job.

You can access this information in a variety of ways. Your local or college library may have copies of these newspapers or magazines. Most print publications have a strong online presence as well. Some require a fee for full access to their articles, while others may be accessed for free. Several Web sites offer full view of magazines online, including Magatopia (www.magatopia.com). Your college or local library might also have access to specific publications through an online library system. When you access these Web sites through your library, the fee may be waived.

On some publications' Web sites you can sign up to receive a daily e-mail containing a short list of key headlines and links to the full article. Individual Web sites will also usually allow you to sign up to receive an RSS (for "rich site summary" or "really simple syndication") feed on key topics. Most Web sites also include podcasts and videos with additional information on key stories and blogs from feature reporters.

There are also several excellent daily e-mail digests—aggregated lists of articles from a variety of publications on various media topics. The digest provides the headline, a short description, and a link to the full story. One such digest is provided by the Benton Foundation. You can sign up to receive this free service at http://www.benton.org. Another site specializing in media news is Cynopsis (www.cynopsis.com). You can sign up for one or more of its three daily digests on digital media, general industry topics, or children's media.

To help you get started, in this section we've categorized publications into three types—newspapers, business and general-interest magazines, and industry and trade publications. Each section contains a list of the major publications in that area and general information about some of the publications listed.

Begin slowly. This is a long list. As you read a particular article, ask yourself, "What information is contained here that might help advance my education and career opportunities?" Copy the most influential articles and add them to your portfolio (from Tip 12, "Keep a Portfolio") or a specific file folder on your computer.

With a newspaper or magazine at one hundred pages or more, it can be challenging to know which headlines will lead to worthwhile stories and which can be passed over. To help cultivate your skill at recognizing media-related articles, some sample headlines are listed below. This is a skill that will dramatically improve with use. After just a week of reading a newspaper or other publications, you'll begin to see themes and it will be easier to decide what's important to you.

Sample Headlines

"Is the iPad Living Up to the Hype?" (telecommunications industry)
"The Changing Bookstore Battle" (publishing)
"Google's Next Ad Frontier May Be in Videogames," "Wii Outsells Playstation in Japan" (video gaming)
"San Francisco to Go Wireless" (cellular industry)
"A Personal Computer to Carry in a Pocket," "Blogging between the Lines" (computers)
"The War Endures, but Where's the Media?" (news)
"Behind the Epidemic of Lousy Viral Campaigns," "U.S. Hispanic Ad Agencies Continue Double-Digit Growth" (advertising)
"Attack of the Zombie Computers Is a Growing Threat" (security)

"Marketers Look to Social Media for Interaction" (business marketing)
"Motown Helps Upstart Miami Label CMG" (music industry)
"ABC Banking on Hourlongs to Capture Ratings Crown" (television)

A. Newspapers
Newspapers recognized as industry leaders include the following.

Boston Globe
Chicago Tribune
Christian Science Monitor
Houston Chronicle
Los Angeles Times
New York Times
Philadelphia Inquirer
St. Petersburg Times
USA Today
Wall Street Journal
Washington Post

Also consider your local newspaper and local business newsweekly.

All newspapers now have a strong online presence. Some, like the *Christian Science Monitor,* have migrated away from publishing daily paper versions and now focus on online content. In fact, newspapers are starting to see themselves more as gatherers of news and information and less as exclusively print-based media companies. Approximately six of the newspapers listed above, including the *New York Times* and *USA Today,* write frequently on media issues. Become familiar with those kinds of papers first.

Wall Street Journal (http://www.wsj.com). The *Wall Street Journal* (*WSJ*) is not only for business majors and working business professionals. Many communications professionals read the *WSJ* daily and use it as one of their primary sources of information—information on which they base important decisions. Get a current issue and look it over. Here are some helpful hints.

By skimming just a few issues of the *WSJ,* you'll find headlines crossing several media topics, including telecommunications, television and cable casting, digital technology, the music industry, the Internet, and legal and ethical issues. A fee is required to read most of the *WSJ* online, so take a look at the print edition for free in your library.

New York Times (http://www.nytimes.com). A wide variety of media-related articles may be found in the *New York Times*. However, each Monday the Business section of the *Times* is devoted to media and advertising issues. This is well worth a look. The Thursday issue includes a section on technology that is especially interesting. Often the entire section is relevant for both media and communications majors because many information companies—particularly those involved in computer-related hardware, software, and data services—seem to be merging or working with communications companies.

Make sure to read the advertisements. If you're interested in public service, look for full-page advertisements sponsored by the Ad Council. The Ad Council produces public service announcements (PSAs) in many media on several different issues. Such an ad may lead you to a place you didn't expect to go, such as involvement in important social issues. The Ad Council's Web site is http://www.ad council.org, and we highly recommend that you take a look at it if you're interested in media with a social conscience. Its brief mission statement on the home page explains exactly what it does: "We marshal the forces of advertising agencies and media companies to effect positive social change."

Just skimming the *New York Times* and then focusing on a few relevant articles will open you up to new avenues to explore. The articles may serve as the basis for a class paper, a senior thesis, an internship, or a job inquiry. Starting in 2011, the *New York Times* will charge for unlimited access to its Web site. While you can still access a small number of articles for free, you can likely view the print paper for free in your library.

Christian Science Monitor (http://www.csmonitor.com). In addition to the standard sections—World, USA, Work & Money, and editorials—the *Christian Science Monitor* has wonderful articles in its Arts & Entertainment, Learning, Innovation, Environment, Books, and Home Forum sections, often with a different perspective than other national papers. The *Christian Science Monitor* prints a weekly magazine and provides comprehensive news coverage on its Web site.

USA Today (http://www.usatoday.com). This national daily provides frequent coverage of media and communications issues and developments in its four major sections: Newsline, Moneyline, Sportsline, and Lifeline. The articles are brief and easy to read. Newsline and Lifeline often have lead stories about pop culture and media; these sections seem to be favorites among the paper's readers. Sportsline includes articles about sports television that offer a critique of television sports coverage and report on new developments, such as plans for new sports channels. Because of its easy-to-read format and frequent attention to pop culture, *USA Today* may be a good place to start your reading; you can expand from there as you become more knowledgeable and develop focused interests. The paper's Web site is colorful, fun to use, and includes content not found in the print version.

Local Newspaper. Although local newspaper circulation has diminished quite a bit over the past ten years, most cities still have a newspaper that covers the local and regional news of the day. Most local newspapers also have a strong online presence. If your goal is to work in the local job market, the local paper should be high on your reading list.

Local Business Newspaper. Many midsize cities (and most large ones) publish at least one business newsweekly. In addition to the articles that cover the area's industries, these papers have a special focus each week, sometimes taking an in-depth look at one industry or topic. A local business paper can be an invaluable resource about people and firms in your area. In an issue focusing on advertising, the paper may list all the agencies in the area, with key personnel, addresses, phone numbers, and the like. These newsweeklies also publish related resource guides. For example, the Web site for *The Business Journals*, a company producing local business newspapers in over forty major U.S. cities, publishes the *Book of Lists*, which lists area businesses by type. This provides useful information that you'll need to contact the companies you're interested in. You will also be able to see—all in one book—how local firms differ in terms of gross sales, number of employees, and so on. To see if there's a book for a city you're interested in, simply go to www.bizjournals.com and click on the "Book of Lists" tab on the top of the screen.

B. Business and General-Interest Magazines

Magazines recognized as industry leaders include the following:

Bloomberg Businessweek
Fast Company
Forbes
Fortune
Newsweek
Time
Wired

Business and general-interest magazines provide in-depth coverage of most communications and media topics. Their articles are often longer than those in a daily newspaper, and they are able to use their less-frequent publication schedule as an opportunity to delve more deeply into topics. Business and general-interest magazines can widen your horizons so that you can more effectively operate in a wide arena. Let's take a quick look at some of these magazines.

Bloomberg Businessweek (http://www.businessweek.com). This weekly magazine provides articles on timely topics from the business perspective. Stories on media companies are often highlighted with information on how the company is planning its growth or dealing with layoffs or customer challenges. The magazine's table of contents and Web site navigation are so well organized and easy to read that you can quickly select articles of interest to you. Subheadings such as Technology, Innovation, Management, Global, Small Business, and Finance lead you to sections that often carry articles about media and communications.

Fortune (http://www.fortune.com). This weekly magazine focuses on the business ups and downs of running a company. Even if you don't plan on owning a business yourself, you'll be working for someone who is. Understanding what drives business success is vital. One issue of *Fortune* was devoted entirely to "the companies, consumers, and innovators shaping the world's hottest economy"—China. China's development is now a common subject in the media, and communications students should pay attention to how this will affect media businesses. The Web site link leads to *Fortune* at CNN Money.com and connects to other useful information on the Web.

Forbes (http://www.forbes.com). Each issue of this semimonthly magazine has several articles providing a business and investor perspective. Occasionally, it covers the media business directly, usually the tech industry. But you'll also find articles on leadership, entrepreneurs, and the economy that connect back to the media business.

Time (http://www.time.com) and *Newsweek* (http://www.newsweek.com). These weekly magazines provide stories with a national and international focus, often touching on technology and business development.

Wired (http://www.wired.com) and *Fast Company* (http://www.fastcompany.com). These two publications focus primarily on innovation, managing a media business, technology, and contemporary approaches to common business issues.

Read whatever magazines you find interesting, and keep reading them. Cultivate your own interests. A good way to expand your knowledge of what is available is to browse through the magazine section of your college library or a large bookstore. You can also search online magazine sites like magatopia.com. Online searches can provide access to a vast assortment of publications. But sometimes only the real-life, visual stimulation of the magazine section of a library or bookstore will do the trick. We often find magazine cover stories about projects that we are currently working on or on topics that interest us. You may have a similar experience finding inspiration in articles that help you with a class project or career decision.

Don't forget to also read the book reviews, editorials, and (again) advertisements. You can learn from all these sections. Another advantage of this type of reading is that it familiarizes you with business terms that are commonly used in the industry and that you may first hear in college classrooms. Seeing those terms in professional publications is proof of how important the terms are in real business situations.

C. Industry and Trade Publications

Depending on your area of specialization, these publications may be of interest:

Advertising Age
AJR: American Journalism Review
Billboard
Broadcasting and Cable
B-to-B
CJR: Columbia Journalism Review
Documentary
Filmmaker
Hollywood Reporter
Info World
Internet Week
Marketing News
Millimeter
Radio World
Real Screen
Variety
Videography

Industry and trade publications are an extremely important category of reading material, and once you get involved in a specific communications field, these may be the most important reading that you do. College students generally do not read these types of publications and often don't even know they're available. But these are the publications that working professionals read. There are far too many trade publications to review in this brief guidebook, but several are highlighted in the following discussion, and their Web addresses are noted. In most cases, the online versions of these magazines are well worth exploring. Many are completely free or have some portions that are free. However, if you don't see your specific interest in this list of publications, talk with your professors, advisers, librarians, and the working professionals you meet for suggestions on what you should read. There's a magazine out there focusing on your interest.

Advertising Age (http://www.adage.com). This publication is essential reading for anyone who is interested in advertising, public relations, direct mail, and commercial production. Moreover, it publishes special issues that focus on the broadcasting, newspaper, or magazine industry. *Advertising Age* is well written and is designed so that almost everyone will find it fascinating. It is recommended reading whatever your field of study.

Advertising Age is divided into sections by media. If you are looking for an article on a particular topic in advertising or public relations, try thumbing through several copies of *Advertising Age*, or do an online search within the site. This will take you on a great trip, and you may find exactly what you want or new topics that you would not have found by searching a reference work such as the *Readers' Guide to Periodical Literature* or even surfing the Web. Resources like the *Readers' Guide* will help with most research needs, but they won't provide references from current issues. Database searches using library tools such as ProQuest or LexisNexis can identify more recent articles. If you don't know about such search tools, talk with a research librarian.

In addition, *Advertising Age* does a wonderful job with special topics such as health care, magazines, radio, and so on. If you happen to come across a special topic in *Advertising Age* that is related to a project you are working on, you will probably find a wealth of helpful information. As is suggested in the earlier section on newspapers, take careful note of the advertising. Ask yourself, "Who is advertising in this publication?" and "What do I think of the ads?" (This activity also connects to Tip 3: "Be a Critical Consumer.") After you have evaluated the ads and read a few articles, scan the back-of-the-magazine sections, such as the classified ads and the business-to-business sections. Other advertising trade publications include *Adweek, Journal of Advertising,* and *Journal of Advertising Research.*

American Journalism Review (AJR) (http://www.ajr.org). *AJR* is a publication of the University System of Maryland Foundation, housed at the Philip Merrill College of Journalism at the University of Maryland. It is a respected industry publication that explores issues important to the field of journalism today by considering the multiple perspectives these complex issues deserve.

AJR also includes advertisements for internship or fellowship opportunities, as does the *Columbia Journalism Review* (discussed later in this section). Examples of the types of topics featured in *AJR* include the state of the newspaper industry, the emergence of online journalism, social media's impact on the news, and ethics in journalism.

Billboard (http://www.billboard.com). *Billboard* focuses primarily on the music and music video businesses and is considered the bible of the music industry. Its music coverage spans creative, technical, and business subjects. The front page is devoted to news and is followed by sections on Artists and Music, International, Merchants and Marketing, Reviews and Previews, Programming, Classified Advertising, and Real Estate. Also included are sections on music genres (such as R&B, Dance, and Rap) that feature articles, editorials, and charts detailing the gross sales of albums, singles, and videos.

Like many other industry trade publications, *Billboard* has great special focus issues, and a wonderful issue called "The Year in Music" is published annually in December. The encyclopedic nature of this newsmagazine makes it enormously useful. Those who want to know what's going on in the music industry need to read *Billboard.* Other music publications worth reading, if this is your field of interest, include *Rolling Stone, Spin,* and *XXL.*

Broadcasting and Cable (http://www.broadcastingcable.com). This popular publication is read throughout the television, cable, radio, multimedia, entertainment, and media-law fields. Sections include Programming, Technology, Washington Watch, People, and Syndication & Distribution. It's well organized and easy to follow. *Broadcasting and Cable* is as important for television and radio majors to read as *Advertising Age* is for advertising, public relations, and marketing majors.

B-to-B: The Magazine for Marketing Strategists (http://www.btobonline
.com). *B-to-B* focuses on the world of business-to-business marketing,
an important segment of the marketing industry that is often not well
known to college students. *B-to-B* has easy-to-read, colorful graphics and
great ads. The online version provides articles and resources, including
a ranking of the best B-to-B Web sites, profiles of the best media buyers
in the business, a listing of the B-to-B top 100 and B-to-B events, an online directory, trade show listings, and more. The site is extremely useful
and well organized.

Columbia Journalism Review (CJR) (http://www.cjr.org). *CJR*'s mission
statement is printed at the top of its contents page: "To assess the performance of journalism . . . to help stimulate continuing improvement
in the profession, and to speak out for what is right, fair, and decent."
Readers find it provocative because *CJR* focuses on issues affecting the
journalism and media industry, not celebrities. Stories cover all aspects
of the field—ethics of reporters, profiles of newsrooms, legal issues, editorial cartoons. Other sections include commentary, book reviews, and
international coverage. *CJR* is an important magazine for all communications majors, but especially journalism majors. Any curious individual
will find this magazine fascinating and useful.

Documentary: The Magazine of the International Documentary Association
(http://www.documentary.org). *Documentary* is a well-respected magazine serving a wide audience—filmmakers, teachers, and others interested in nonfiction film. Each month's issue carries a feature article and
has a special focus, such as documentaries that focus on music or nature.
Other articles cover legal issues, technology, and profiles of producers.
It's a great read and will appeal to anyone with a filmmaking interest.

Filmmaker: The Magazine of Independent Film (http://www.filmmakermagazine
.com). *Filmmaker* features interviews with renowned independent filmmakers, feature articles on trends and new techniques, film reviews, and
an Industry Beat column. A recent issue included a special report on the
Sundance Film Festival and a feature on how DIY (do-it-yourself) filmmakers became their own distributors to get their movies shown to audiences.
In addition, its Web site features interactive forums, business resources for
filmmaking, calendars of indie film festivals, podcasts, and a blog.

Hollywood Reporter (http://www.hollywoodreporter.com). This is a must
read for anyone interested in the feature-film and network-television in-

dustries. It gives the inside word on current and upcoming projects and the people involved. It also covers key issues on topics such as copyright and fair use, union contracts for online content, and special features on the Academy Awards. Unfortunately, because the *Hollywood Reporter* is expensive, many libraries do not subscribe to it. However, even checking its Web site can provide insights into current industry issues.

Infoworld (http://www.infoworld.com). This publication is directed at business-minded people interested in how technologies work and how they can use new technologies in their businesses. *Infoworld* includes a varied mix of articles and topics, from computer operating systems and the public reaction to the latest iPhone to updates on antitrust cases against software giants.

Internet Week (http://www .internetwk.com). With the slogan "technology that connects the enterprise," this publication has an e-commerce emphasis and often covers advertising, marketing, and media as they relate to Internet businesses. It commonly covers Net infrastructure and wireless technology news updates. In addition, *Internet Week* provides in-depth articles on such subjects as broadband and online video, as well as reviews of new products and services. This magazine is especially useful to entrepreneurs and new media professionals.

Marketing News (http://www.marketingpower.com/AboutAMA/Pages /AMA%20Publications/Marketing%20News/MarketingNews.aspx). This is a publication of the American Marketing Association. It is similar in style and size to *Advertising Age* and *Broadcasting and Cable*, but not as glitzy and with fewer photos and graphics. Field experts write columns on a variety of important subjects such as marketing and the law, integrated marketing, and advertising to businesses. Specific issues of *Marketing News* review the year in marketing, new trends, and best and worst practices. A quick Stats column in one issue lays out the top four deficiencies in new marketing hires—analytical skills, specialized education, ability to improve analytical abilities, and search engine marketing skills. If you skim through other issues, you will find lists of marketing firms organized by type. These profile lists can be helpful for your research, whether it's for a class assignment or a job search.

Millimeter (http://www.digitalcontentproducer.com). This monthly magazine and its vast online site covers technology, techniques, and talent across the spectrum of film, television, and video production—for all applications and all screens.

Radio World (http://www.rwonline.com). This is a news source for radio managers and engineers. In addition to a printed magazine, the Web site provides a rich mix of resources and articles. This central Web site for *Radio World Newspapers* has an international focus. There are four corresponding print publications: *Radio World Newspaper*, U.S. edition; *Radio World International*, covering Europe, the Middle East, Africa, Asia, Canada, the Caribbean, and the Pacific; *Radio World América Latina*, covering South and Central America and Mexico; and Radio World *édition francophone*, covering France and all French-speaking territories. These four regional publications reach professionals in many different languages across hundreds of different countries. The site also links you directly to other Web sites and publications of *Radio World*'s parent company, New Bay Media: *TV Technology* (http://www.TVtechnology .com), *Videography* (www.videography.com) and *Government Video* (www .governmentvideo.com).

Real Screen (http://www.realscreen.com). This magazine states it is "about the business of Docs, Infomags and Lifestyle programming," appealing mostly to filmmakers and content creators who want to produce for television and cable entities such as PBS, A&E, Discovery, National Geographic, P.O.V., Sundance, and the like. *Real Screen* is both nationally and internationally oriented, focusing on linking filmmakers with major distribution outlets and highlighting opportunities outside the United States.

Variety (http://www.variety.com). If you're interested in the world of feature films or network television, *Variety* is a weekly magazine worth reading (in print or online) regularly. Variety tracks the gross receipts of the movie industry as well as deals involving independent filmmakers, national cable programmers, syndicators, and distributors—the business that emanates from Hollywood and New York. It also covers music, the Internet, and even has a section on theater titled "Legit." *Variety* is famous for its witty (and often biting) writing style. Like *Billboard*, it's fun to read.

Articles provide not only an inside view into the entertainment industry but also the names of people starting new jobs and new ventures. This is a great way to research new job opportunities. Students who are interested in working in these fields would be wise to record the names of key people in this publication for future reference.

Videography (http://www.videography.com). This is a very good monthly publication for those interested in video production and postproduction, uses of computers in video, new developments in equipment (such as digital cameras, lighting, graphics, and animation), and international production. It is directed at nonbroadcast videographers, producers, and editors who earn their livelihood in the world of corporate communications as well as a wide variety of broadcast producers who work in television or at commercial production houses in what the magazine calls "the content creation community." *Videography* covers new technology well, often providing a perspective as to how it can help the small business owner.

These are just a few of the valuable industry trade and specialty publications. Look for the ones in your specialty and try to read at least one regularly. Don't be afraid to browse. Visit their Web sites for articles, podcasts, and reporter's blogs.

30. LEARN ABOUT COMPANY BUDGETS

Communications businesses make money in very specific ways—for example, by licensing content to new distribution outlets, by creating original content for unique media, by collecting commissions when purchasing advertising time, and by selling advertising time. There are also flat fees for creating products, writing proposals, and so on. Whether or not your internship or job requires you to understand budgeting, this is a skill worth learning.

Your college coursework, particularly upper-level courses, can help with this, but often colleges don't teach the conservative attitude toward money and budgets that exists in media businesses. Overhead and profit are considered at every turn. In most cases, media businesses are labor intensive, meaning that most of the expenses are incurred in hiring *people*, not purchasing things. Small mistakes in budgeting may wipe out the profit or even turn a project into a money loser. Not knowing the ins and outs of how your firm budgets is a big mistake. Built into the rates and charges of media companies are assumptions about the time that it takes to accomplish particular tasks, appropriate delivery systems, and proper return-on-investment (ROI). All of this means that exceeding a budget or failing to keep track of costs can be dangerous. On the other hand, a healthy grasp of budgeting can help propel you to more responsibility and better projects. Take the time to learn the business model of your company and how it budgets, and be able to "talk the talk" when necessary.

31. SMALL TASKS CAN EQUAL BIG REWARDS

Taking on small tasks that show your willingness to pitch in will advance you into better jobs faster. Become known as the person who will "get the job done," whether that job is filing a stack of papers, organizing the equipment room, or staying late to help collate the handouts for tomorrow's important presentation. Sure, the big tasks are more exciting and look good on your ever-growing resumé, but the small tasks are often the ones that are most appreciated by your boss. And remember, your boss holds the key to your promotion, raise, or ability to get those big assignments.

That small-task list should even include something as seemingly unimportant as making coffee. If you are serving an internship and see a harried professional making coffee every morning, you could make yourself famous in an instant. Offer to make the coffee, and then do it every day. Have you merely shown an amazing sensitivity by making coffee? No, you've gone one better. You've shown that you recognize that the professional's time is valuable. If you take on a small task, it allows that person to get to work sooner. It will be appreciated.

As a personal example, one afternoon James Seguin, one of the authors of this guide, asked a new employee to deliver some materials to a client. Her response was, "Well, I don't want to do that right now. The traffic's really heavy." That was the wrong answer. This may have been a small task, but the importance of it was massive. Maybe she didn't know that—but James did. His response was, "The client needs the tapes now, and it's either you or me. So you'd better get going." Her remark had demonstrated an unwillingness to do what was needed—unless someone pushed her. To her credit, she never did that again, and she became a great worker. Other small tasks may lead to big rewards:

- Know the area where you live and work, and be able to drive around and find places on your own so you're ready when the need arises. If that means studying a city map at night or investing in a GPS, do it.
- Be more than punctual: Be early.
- Learn the ins and outs of the office equipment in your particular office—fax machines, computers, and photocopiers. Be able and willing to do the small fixes that are often necessary.

ON THE JOB: Present Your Best Features

Be yourself. Don't lie (we will find out everything about you eventually). And do not sell yourself short. Drop the sense of "entitlement." Too many recent college grads or folks with little experience walk in expecting to be well-paid, work short hours, and have an active work/social life.

John Barra
TV producer

- Say yes when asked if you can work overtime and on weekends. Both are common and expected. Working overtime or weekend hours can have the added bonus of putting you in a different work environment or situation with your supervisor, other colleagues, or people from a completely different department.

32. DEVELOP A POSITIVE ATTITUDE AND PASSION

Personal attributes matter more when people are hiring than almost anything else. If a person is competent and knowledgeable, he or she certainly has the foundation required for good work. But a lack of proper attitude and passion infiltrates all phases of a person's life like a disease. What good are intelligence and skill if they are not applied, or are applied without the diligence, stamina, and positive attitude needed in the workplace? Given the choice, most employers would rather teach someone with a strong work ethic the ins and outs of a job than hire a person who already knows the work, but has a lackadaisical attitude. They know that a person who consistently works hard will do a job well once he or she knows how to do it. A person who cares is consistently reliable. Attitude and passion don't come easily. If going to college is your work, then your attitude and passion for what you do will bring you good grades and positive recommendations when you graduate. These attributes mean that you maintain high standards even under duress, that you never give up, and that you find a way to solve problems. If you can develop these attributes in college, you will be a leader and well prepared for the world of work that demands these qualities daily.

Being positive may be difficult for some people, so if you can consistently present a reasonably positive attitude, you will stand out. We say "reasonably" because an artificial, overly positive attitude is not appropriate. Negative attitudes abound everywhere and they're a waste of time and energy. However, finding ways to maintain a positive attitude through difficult times takes effort. We suggest you read at least one of Stephen R. Covey's books, such as *The Seven Habits of Highly Effective People, Principle-Centered Leadership,* or *First Things First: To Live, to Love, to Learn, to Leave a Legacy.* These books discuss positive attitudes, trustworthiness, and much more. You can find them in most libraries and bookstores.

33. BE TRUSTWORTHY

To be trustworthy means exactly that—to be worthy of someone's trust. Being trustworthy in all aspects of your life is necessary for you to be successful. In a professional environment, trustworthiness means that coworkers or supervisors can count on you no matter what the circumstances. It means being true to your word and doing what you said you'd do, when you said you'd do it. Trustworthiness speaks to your character—to the core of who you are and what you stand for. As stated previously, some skills can be taught. But trustworthiness cannot. Valued interns and employees convey their trustworthiness in many ways—by refraining from gossip and mean conversations about coworkers, by being true to their word at all times, by not putting themselves in situations that could be misinterpreted, and by seeking opportunities to support their company and coworkers honestly and with integrity.

34. DON'T BURN YOUR BRIDGES

When something goes wrong for you on the job (and it certainly will)— something as simple as an argument over who got the better office space or as complicated as conflicting views over the direction of a project— it's easy to want to lash out at the people who you feel are being unfair to you. We often become emotionally involved in our work and resent those who interfere. Tempers flare, and relationships can be damaged. Sometimes the argument is more serious and can result in movement to a new section of the company, failure to get a promotion, or even a layoff. Regardless, you must be able to remain professional and keep aggressive comments and behaviors out of the workplace.

Because people working in the media industry tend to jump from media company to media company, you can expect to keep running into the same people. It's always best to patch up differences and leave a company on good terms. Badmouthing your former bosses and colleagues (especially in job interviews) will come back to haunt you when you least expect it.

35. BECOME AWARE OF CORPORATE CULTURE

If you think that understanding corporate culture is a bit of a puzzle, you're not alone. It can take months or years to understand fully an organization's culture. You may find this to be true in trying to understand the culture of your college department, your dorm, and your family, as well as in your workplace. It's a puzzle because the rituals, stories, and regulations that make up corporate culture are not written down, openly recognized, or discussed, yet everyone in the organization seems to know what they are and when they are being violated. You can learn about corporate culture by being a good listener and observer. For example, attendance at holiday parties may be regarded as mandatory even though the invitation implies otherwise. Overtime may be expected, particularly for newly hired employees. Dress is a part of corporate culture. Corporate culture is not something to be afraid of, but it is something that you need to be sensitive to so that if you choose not to conform to it, you will be doing so by choice, not by accident.

Participation is an area that often reflects a workplace culture. Let's say that you are an intern at an ad agency and you are invited to sit in on a brainstorming meeting. Before the meeting starts, people begin telling funny stories about work-related incidents. Should you tell one? Probably not. You're not really a participant in this meeting: You're an attendee. You are not in a position to hold up the meeting or dominate attention. The joking and chatter often have meaning beyond the moment. Even if it's not on a conscious level, a good deal of positioning is being done through joking and storytelling. For example, someone might tell a story about a project that he worked on at a previous company and how it ran into serious problems, how he stayed up all night to meet the deadline, and how everyone loved the final result. These "saved-the-day" stories are typical and are enjoyed by others because they have had similar experiences. The *real* story is that these anecdotes establish the employee's competence, stamina, and commitment to excellence. Let them do that. Your job is to listen, learn, and enjoy.

However, if you're asked to research a topic, produce initial storyboards, or write drafts, you are definitely being regarded as a participant and should begin your work immediately. In most cases, asking questions as you go is fine. But if you are uncomfortable with an assigned task—because you haven't done it before (perhaps they think you have) or you don't know where to start—make that known immediately. Most communications work is produced on a tight schedule, and waiting makes things worse. Professionals often forget that experience has taught them how to accomplish work quickly and productively. This means that an open and comfortable relationship—one in which you can express your concerns and ask questions—is best for you.

Participation in organized outside-of-work activities is often worthwhile. For example, if the company is planning its annual community day (when employees provide community services such as helping the elderly or painting houses), offer to take part. If you are invited to join others for lunch, arrange your schedule and finances so that it's possible for you to attend. People will get to know you in a different way, and you will begin to see what you have in common with people who may be quite different from you. You may even meet someone who can be a mentor.

To understand your company's culture, start by observing the day-to-day environment. Here are some questions to keep in mind.

- When do people normally arrive at and leave work?
- What's a typical daily or weekly workload? Does it normally involve evenings and weekends?
- What is the quality of work that is produced and what are the criteria on which the work is judged? Evaluate both in your own mind.
- How do people react to stress?
- How is conflict handled?
- How do people balance their work and outside-of-work pursuits?
- How do people dress?
- What attitudes are shown toward women and minorities?

All of these questions will help you decipher the corporate culture at your workplace. Remember, corporate culture is different in each workplace, so you'll want to ask these questions each time your workplace changes.

36. DEVELOP MENTORS

Mentors are people who have achieved some level of success and are willing to meet and work with you to assist your progress from student to success in your chosen career. Many students are afraid to become friendly with people who are in successful positions, but avoiding such people or failing to cultivate relationships with them is a mistake. Become comfortable with people who are older and who are in prestigious or interesting positions, including professors, older students who are working and attending classes, graduate students, people you meet on your summer jobs or during field visits, guest speakers to your class, people you meet when you attend a professional organization's meetings, parents of friends, neighbors, and others. Some people enjoy helping a student learn about an industry or a particular opportunity. Convey an interest in learning about an area or an interest in improving your situation. If you show your motivation, people will be more likely to help you.

Making connections is the first step. When you do establish relationships, don't forget to follow up. That means thanking individuals in writing, but it also means staying in touch. You can do this through occasional phone calls or e-mails. You can do more than thank people. Once you know of someone's interests, you may find newspaper or magazine articles that you feel are of interest to that individual: Send them on with a note. Or simply keep someone informed of your progress.

To do any of this, you need a foolproof method of keeping good records—back to that professional contact list again (see Tip 4, "Start a Professional Contact List"). Make sure you have a file with names, addresses, phone numbers, and e-mail addresses. Take notes on what you discussed; keep track of people's interests, children, and hobbies. This doesn't mean being a snoop or a stalker; it means showing a sincere interest in people. Developing mentors takes a bit of self-analysis and guts. You need to know your own strengths and weaknesses; a mentor can help you improve in weak areas if you are willing to discuss such things. Mentors can refer you to other people or give you advice on how to handle a difficult situation.

Mentors are important once you are in a job, too. Many work situations are difficult for new employees. Often, personal and business paths can cross in odd directions: You may need advice on an ethical problem, for example. Sometimes, even veterans find it hard to know what to do. If you have a trusted mentor, you can talk and figure out a plan. This can be invaluable for those who want to progress steadily up the ladder to jobs with more responsibility and higher pay.

37. LEARN TO NETWORK

Finding a mentor, finding a job at your dream company, finding professional success—all are served by knowing how to network. Networking is really about making friends and connections from one friend to another. Early in your career, you'll need networking contacts who are willing to help you—but as your career progresses, you'll find that you can help others as well. It's the give and take that makes a successful networker.

Networkers sometimes get a bad rap and can be seen as opportunists with insincere motives. But successful networkers are neither. They like to meet new people and enjoy learning about their interests and career paths. We see networking as a four-step process—connect, listen, record, reconnect. Meeting someone is the connect part. This could happen in person, or online through a social networking site. Networking through friends of friends is particularly easy on these Web sites; in fact, that's their purpose—connecting those with similar interests and passions to one another. While using sites like Facebook to make business connections may seem like an easy extension of your college days, be conscious of the difference between Web sites meant to connect "friends" versus Web sites with the express purpose of making business connections (such as LinkedIn). You may notice that other people blur the lines between friends and professional contacts. However, early in your career, it's a good idea to respect those differences. Keep your business networking on a business networking Web site and your friends on a different site. (Although, with online searching as easy as it is, even if you direct someone to your professional site, that person may find your personal site as well. It's best never to put anything online that you wouldn't want a potential employer to see.) After you've established a connection with someone in-person or online, listening, talking, and sharing are part two of the networking process. Step three is record—putting that information into a professional contact list so that it can be referred to later. And getting back in touch with that person at a later time, or reconnecting, is step four.

Get comfortable with talking to people about yourself and asking about them. Prepare your "elevator speech"—a short series of sentences about yourself that you can rattle off in the time that it takes for a typical elevator ride. Commit the speech to memory and be ready to share it the next time you're in a networking situation and someone says, "Hi. What do you do?"

38. BE INDISPENSABLE

If you want your internship or first job to yield you the best reference possible, be indispensable. Being competent is the first step to success. But lots of people are competent. If you want to be the person who is offered the best opportunities, you need to go one step further and be indispensable.

What does it mean to be indispensable in an internship or job? It means being the person who is always there to help, in whatever way is needed, with a positive attitude and a smile. It means being more knowl-edgeable than those around you expect you to be, being more willing than might be necessary, and being humble about your personal success and boastful about the team. It means showing up ahead of everyone else so that you're always ready to help. Or staying late. It means an-ticipating needs, rather than merely asking, "What can I do?" Although busy people need help, they're often not good at stopping what they're doing in the frantic pace of the moment and turning to an available per-son nearby to delegate a task that could help alleviate their angst.

If there's a big shoot tomorrow, you can ask the producer, "What can I do?"—or you can say "Do you need me to pick up food?," "Does any-one on the crew or any talent need to be given a ride or to be picked up at the train station?," or "Do you need me to stop at the office in the morning to get any last-minute materials?" If you see your boss staying late with papers piled high on his or her desk, it means offering, "Would you like me to organize or file those papers?," "Is there any report or article I could read for you and write up a brief overview?," or "Would you like me to start on the PowerPoint for next week's presentation?" Asking targeted questions such as these shows that you understand how the workplace runs and the kinds of "to do" items that can pile up for a busy person.

6

SEIZE YOUR ENTREPRENEURIAL SPIRIT

Whether you consider yourself an entrepreneur or not, finding ways to act in an innovative, enterprising, business-savvy manner can be beneficial to your career growth. Entrepreneurs show initiative, are solution-oriented, and are effective risk takers. Successful entrepreneurs may attempt a business venture that unveils a new invention or idea, but they do so with considerable thought, research, and planning. Consider these tips for invigorating your entrepreneurial spirit.

39. APPLY FOR GRANTS AVAILABLE TO STUDENTS

Check your department and dorm bulletin board or Web site and you will occasionally find organizations offering a grant for a student to develop and produce a communications product. This is a wonderful opportunity and something worth considering, particularly in your junior or senior year.

For example, the University Film and Video Association offers the Carole Fielding Student Grants (http://www.ufva.org/grants/fielding), which award anywhere from $1,000 to $4,000 for different types of film, video, or multimedia productions. Categories include documentary, narrative, experimental, multimedia, and animation. This project requires a proposal, but completing the application requirements (such as purpose statement, audience, schedule, and budget) is a worthwhile experience. If you were to receive such a grant and complete a high-quality project, it would be extremely beneficial—both for your resumé and as a learning experience. The Broadcast Education Association (BEA) (http://www.beaweb.org) offers several scholarships for communications and media students, including the Two-Year/Community College BEA Awards, the Walter S. Patterson Scholarship, and the Abe Voron Scholarship. Some of these awards offer up to $5,000. For details, visit the BEA Web site, or ask a professor in television/video or broadcasting to assist you. Finally, don't overlook your own school for grant funds. Many offer competitive grants for students to develop their own projects and then work tirelessly to publicize those projects once completed. It's like having your own PR firm. Completing a project for your own school may open up opportunities for letters of recommendation from instructors involved in the program and serving in a mentoring role for your project. If you have a great idea for a project and the drive to complete it, there is nothing to lose by applying for such opportunities!

40. TAKE AN INDEPENDENT STUDY

If there is a project you would like to complete or if you have a specific area of interest but no course is offered in that area, consider taking an independent or directed study. By doing so, you could work with one professor (often of your choice) and pursue your specialty. Independent study is a good way to work with a professor whose professional expertise you would like to learn and draw from. It can also be a path toward getting published or drafting an initial business plan to help you develop your own business idea.

41. USE THE WEB TO EXPERIMENT WITH A NEW BUSINESS IDEA

Think you have a terrific new media or communications idea? Looking for an inexpensive way to publicize this great idea—or just yourself? Then come up with a clever moniker, buy the domain name, and get a Web site up and running. The Internet is an excellent place to test out your ideas. As we mentioned earlier in Tip 13, "Create a Personal Web Page," if you haven't purchased the domain name of your own name yet, you absolutely should. If your actual name isn't available, get the closest, most memorable alternative. It's inexpensive and well worth the cost. If you have a great name for a new business, purchase that domain name as well.

Your Web site may function simply as a repository of your best work, demo tapes, portfolio items, or well-received papers. But it can also introduce a completely new business idea. And for little cost, you can see if the idea generates "viral" interest. Plus, it shows initiative, skill, and creativity to a potential employer.

Do not post these ideas on your MySpace, Facebook, or other social networking page. These pages are public spaces: Employers check them. Even if you attempt to keep your page professional, it's still not the place to experiment with a new business idea or help potential employers see you as the best candidate for a job. Social networking sites are regarded as informal spaces. If you have a business idea, behave like a real entrepreneur, and set up a real business Web site.

42. START YOUR OWN BUSINESS

If you've got a great idea and a self-starting personality, you might be ready to jump in and start your own business. Smaller, more mobile technologies and lower-cost computer programs have transformed many media ideas from dreams into reality on a smaller budget than you might think. Starting a video production company, for example, used to mean spending hundreds of thousands of dollars on cameras, editing equipment, and animation software. Today, many of those same tasks can be accomplished using software already included with most computers. However, starting a business is not for everyone. Making such a commitment means doing the varied jobs required to run a business either by yourself or with a small team. If embarking on such a journey sparks your intellectual curiosity and entrepreneurial drive, then you may have found your niche.

The best place to start on this path is in a classroom. Does your college or university offer a course in business planning, entrepreneurship, or small-business marketing? Take it! Some, such as Temple University, have a small-business institute in addition to offering entrepreneurial courses in the business school and communication school. If your school doesn't offer such choices, ask about them. Temple University added more of these programs after noticing how often undergraduates mentioned "self-employed" as their current job. With enough demand, your school may respond. College coursework can introduce you to effective business plan development, the means to raise capital or funding, and even self-employed alumni who've made their own business ideas work. Also, many cities have small-business divisions within their local government that provide templates for business planning and budgeting, not to mention the various forms required for starting a business.

While there are many ways to learn the multitude of tasks needed to start a new business, other elements aren't so easily taught. Some people are born with an "entrepreneurial personality," a natural mix of adventurer and risk-taker—common characteristics used to describe those who start their own business. However, don't confuse risk-taking with gambling. Successful entrepreneurs research their ideas, size up the competition, plan for the long haul, and surround themselves with talented help. They don't wake up one morning thinking, "I've got a great idea for a ground-breaking video game" and toss their life savings into a new product launch with a friend by week's end.

If you're considering this path, remember that honest self-assessment will help you enormously as you try to reach your business goal. If you think your idea has the potential to go the distance, then ask yourself, "Am I the best one to move this idea forward? Do I have the personality and drive to make it happen? Do I have either access to money or the skill to bring others with money to the table to make this idea a reality?" (For more ideas on accessing funds for students, see Tip 39, "Apply for Grants Available to Students.") If the answer to all of these questions is "Yes," then you may have found a new and exciting route to professional success.

7

COVER LETTERS, RESUMÉS, AND THANK-YOU NOTES

This chapter contains guidelines for writing cover letters, resumés, and thank-you notes, as well as samples of each. It is important (and easy) to customize cover letters and resumés depending on the company, position, qualifications stated on the job posting, or person with whom you'll be meeting. There is no excuse for delivering a cover letter or resumé that does not take these specifics into account. While it's definitely worthwhile to draft a cover letter and resumé that you consider your "basic version," you should take the time to customize each whenever possible.

Your cover letter, resumé, and thank-you note serve three distinct purposes. Your cover letter should explain, in narrative form, why you are the right person for this particular job, at this particular place, and are worth a face-to-face interview (or whatever may be the appropriate next step). In most cases, your resumé doesn't get you the job; instead, it grabs the interest of the person who is reviewing resumés enough to invite you in for a face-to-face meeting. If you're giving your resumé to someone during the actual interview, its purpose is to remind that person of your qualifications once you leave. Finally, your thank-you note reminds the interviewer why you are the right person for this particular job. A thank-you note is also the right place to help remind the interviewer of ways that your interview was unique or something that you shared in common—perhaps your common interest in chess, an industry leader you both admire, or your similar taste in music.

Below are a few tips to help you get started drafting these documents. It's worth noting that guidelines for cover letters and resumés are as unique as the people doing the hiring. With that in mind, you should take the following tips as guidelines, rather than rules. Not every tip will be right for every situation, but these tips can guide a successful job hunt.

TIPS FOR WRITING COVER LETTERS, RESUMÉS, AND THANK-YOU NOTES

COVER LETTERS

- Get to the point quickly. State the job for which you are applying in the first or second sentence.
- State why you are the right candidate for the job and worth meeting.
- If you've been referred to this job or person by a mentor or other person, name that person in the very first sentence (for example, "I'm writing to you at the recommendation of John Ross").
- Include specific information about the company so that the reader is clear that you don't just want a job—you want a job at *their* company!
- If there is a job posting, reference all the items mentioned in the posting using the same terms that are found in the posting.
- Provide information in the final paragraph about the best way to reach you.
- If possible, state when you will follow up.
- Keep your cover letter to no more than one page.

But the most important point to remember is that your cover letter should reflect what *you* can do *for* the business or organization—not what *it* can do for you. A cover letter should talk about fulfilling the company's needs, not yours. This is the most frequent (and biggest) mistake that people make in cover letters. Stating that "This job is exactly the kind of job I've been looking for" is a statement about you. It's more persuasive to say, "If you need someone to help your company achieve its goal of (STATE GOAL), I have the skills and enthusiasm to help make that happen."

RESUMÉS

The most important resumé tip is: Don't lie—ever. It's not worth the risk. We know someone who was fired after three weeks on the job as soon as the Human Resources Department finally got around to checking the details on her resumé and discovered that she had lied about a key fact. Be creative in how you state something—but don't lie on your resumé. In general, resumés include information based on the following categories.

Resumé Categories and Tips

- *Education:* If your education is the strongest item on your resumé, place it toward the top of the page. However, if you have solid work experience, move education to the bottom of the page. Employers tend to be most interested in your work experience. If you have not yet graduated, simply state that—for example, "Anticipated graduation June 2013." This section is also the place to list relevant classes or coursework. Once you have obtained a college degree of any kind, you should omit any mention of your high school.

- *Work experience:* This is a list of former or current jobs that relate directly to the job you seek. Include your job title, place of employment, years of employment, and your responsibilities in that job. Try to include information that illustrates how your work at that company helped achieve the goals of the company (such as "Increased sales 2 percent," "Reorganized stockroom for greater efficiency," or "Responded to customer requests in a timely manner" rather than "Sold clothes," "Worked in stockroom," or "Answered phones").

- *Related experience:* This is a list of former jobs that reflect an industrious work ethic but may not specifically relate to the job you're applying for. Consider full-time, part-time, unpaid, and paid work. These considerations are especially important if you are a recent college graduate or returning to work after time away.

- *Awards:* List these separately *only* if they illustrate your recent skills and abilities at a high level. Edit the list so that you include only the most impressive items. If you have only one or two awards to mention, omit this section and mention the awards with the associated jobs (or, if it's an education award, move it to your education section).

- *Skills:* These are areas in which you possess a serious proficiency. Basic word-processing skills (such as use of Word, Excel, and PowerPoint software programs) do not qualify for mention. However, industry-specific specialty software programs might. Other skills include typing speed, editing with a particular software program, and related media skills (such as music production, theater stage management, or performance experience).

- *Interests:* These are areas in which you have achieved a high level of skill or ample experience but that fall outside of a typical work experience list. Items might include accomplished pianist for ten years, cardiopulmonary resuscitation certified, numerous musical theater lead roles, amateur race car driver, professional gospel singer, gourmet cook, or serial entrepreneur who has started five successful businesses to raise funds for college. These are items that illustrate your creativity, your industrious nature, or just how fascinating a person you are. They are also often used as conversation starters in job interviews.

You may have noticed that we did not include the category of "goal" or "objective." A stated goal or objective at the top of your resumé is now considered undesirable. If it's there, take it out. Your goal or objective is a statement about *your* needs—not the employer's needs. You are here to serve the employer, not the other way around. A goal or an objective that is reworded to fit the employer's perspective might belong in your cover letter, but not in your resumé.

Resumés Submitted Online

More and more employers are requiring prospective employees to submit their resumés online. Sometimes, this will just mean saving your resumé as a PDF file so it can be uploaded and read easily. In other situations, the employer will require that you plug your information into pre-configured and pre-sized boxes and spaces.

It's important to remember why employers are doing this. Mainly, it makes it easy for the people reviewing resumés to compare them point by point. If everyone submitting a resumé has a limit of twenty words to describe any one job, it makes it much easier for the reviewer to compare experiences. It also means the employer won't have to (or won't get to) read information that you deem important but for which no space is provided, such as "other skills or interests." While this can work very well for employers by helping them compare resumés from a variety of candidates, we think there's actually less benefit to you. However, this method is growing in popularity, so it's worth considering the unique needs of submitting a resumé in this manner. If you've spent time and thought configuring your printed resumé with easy-to-read bullet points, take the time to reformat or reword your information so it will be uploaded and conveyed in the most positive manner. If the site provides helpful hints, read them. An employer's online submission form may be quite different from submitting to a Web site like Monster.com. Learn the nuances of both. And most important of all, be sure to review your submission information one last time before hitting that "Submit" button.

Resumé Writing Style

- Omit personal pronouns; refrain from using *I* language.
- Start sentences with action words (such as "Managed," "Increased," or "Developed").

- Write in short sentences or phrases. Write in a bulleted style rather than a narrative style. (Sentence fragments are acceptable here.)
- Use quantitative examples wherever possible (for example, "Sold 100 jackets in three hours").
- Show how your presence at the job made things better. (For example, don't just say "Typing and filing," but say "Reorganized resource library for more efficient retrieval.")
- Cite specific examples and statistics.
- Keep a consistent tense.
- If you are still doing a particular job, put all information about that job in the present tense.
- If you are no longer at a job, put all information in past or present tense—but be consistent throughout your resumé.

Resumé Visual Style

- At this point in your career, your resumé should absolutely not exceed one page.
- Keep font simple and consistent—around 10- or 12-point font size.
- Keep colors simple and easy to read. You don't know the condition of your readers' eyesight.
- Refrain from unnecessary use of bold, italics, and underlining.
- We read from left to right, so put the most important information either center or to the left and the least important information (such as dates) to the right.

Resumé References

- Don't include references in your basic resumé unless you are asked to do so by your interviewer or you have a reference that could dramatically improve your chances to get the job or the interview.
- Create a separate document that lists your references. Bring it with you during interviews so that you can share it if asked.
- If the job posting requests that references be included, put them on a separate page.
- For each person listed, state your relationship to that person and the length of time that you have known one another.
- Aim high. Ask the highest-ranking or -titled people that you know to be your references.
- Ask your references directly what they will say if called and asked about you. It's okay to tell your references specifically what you need them to say every time you think they will be contacted.
- Tell your references that they are listed on your reference sheet.

- If a specific company is about to call your references, call each person on your list and provide details about the position, its responsibilities, and the things that you need them to say about you.

Resumé Form versus Content

- Be professional first and creative second. You don't know who will be reading your resumé or cover letter or anything about their sense of humor or artistic taste.

Students often worry about the form of the resumé more than its content. They wonder, "Should I list my education or work experience first? Should this be in bold and that in italics?" These questions should be considered, but your time will be better spent finding a way to present your information clearly, honestly, and in a way that puts your best foot forward.

Although it may be true that there's nothing you know better than your own life, it's still difficult to evaluate your own life experiences and determine what parts are appropriate to include in your resumé. Therefore, get help. You do not need to spend thousands of dollars on a resumé coach: Start with your friends. Review each other's resumés. Ask for critical feedback from a professor or trusted mentor. It's much easier to do this on a resumé that's not your own. Friends and mentors can provide feedback about whether your resumé communicates the right message about you, whether it contains the best information (or is missing it!), and whether your attempt at humor is working.

If you find that the first draft of your resumé is boring or unfocused, don't worry about it. That's how you start. Just keep working on it. Remember, your resumé is only a snippet of relevant material presented in a way that is easy to understand, interesting to read—and gets you an interview.

In this chapter, you will find three sample cover letters and three thank-you notes to help guide you when drafting your own. But the chapter's seven sample student resumés will probably be the most useful models for you as you prepare to search for a job. Each resumé was written for a different area of communications. Note that these resumés have different formats, but each emphasizes work experiences, internships, community involvement, and awards. Each one also has a single focus and a pleasing look and is easy for an employer to read—or even skim. Some of the resumés are longer than others. If you have an exceptional story to tell from your college and related experiences, share it briefly in your cover letter. You can always elaborate in the interview.

ON THE JOB: Show Your Enthusiasm

Communicate that you really want the job. It's amazing how few candidates ever express the fact that they really want the job being discussed. Show this by being prepared. Have questions ready. Know about the company and the people who work there.

Be sure to mind your manners. The simple things can make a big difference. Be polite to everyone you meet—from the parking lot attendant to the office administrator. Say please and thank you. Be prepared to make small talk. Turn off your phone completely. Don't interrupt. And send a written thank-you note when you get home.

Amy Caples
College professor and former news anchor

Note that all the resumés included here fit on one page. Part of what keeps a resumé tightly focused is what you leave out. Use the above list to help you critically evaluate your resumé and determine what to include and what to leave out.

Finally, as you're reading the resumés later in this chapter, note the kinds of experiences that these students sought during their college years. Their hard work is paying off and giving them resumés that will attract attention and land them job interviews. Excellent samples of cover letters can also be found in *The Everything Cover Letter Book* by Burton Jay Nadler and on numerous online sites. This book and other helpful references are listed in the Additional Resources section at the back of the book.

THANK-YOU NOTES

Write one! Yes, we may live in a fast-paced, technocentric society, but this is all the more reason to take the time to tell your job interviewer or informational interviewer or anyone else who helps you in your job search—"Thanks." The most memorable thank-you notes are handwritten and mailed within twenty-four hours of the meeting. Build this commitment into your schedule (i.e., write in your datebook, "Meet Jim at noon. Write and mail thank-you note by 5 PM."). If, however, your handwriting is atrocious, type the note.

Invest in professionally boxed, graphically interesting (but simple) thank-you cards. They can be found in any drugstore. Cards with funny pet photos or other comic images are not appropriate. You may make an exception only if your interviewer specifically mentioned their love of these types of cards. An e-mailed thank-you note is acceptable, but makes nowhere near the impression of a handwritten note.

Your note is meant to be a thank you, not a pitch for the job. Remind the person of something pleasantly memorable from the meeting, or share something from the meeting that made an impact on you. You could share new information about something you read about the company or the department. Mention how much you're looking forward to further conversations about the position if you must, but resist the temptation to elaborate on why you are the right candidate for the job. Say thank you, add a few pleasantries, and sign off.

SAMPLE RESUMÉS
PUBLIC RELATIONS

Joseph P. Spektor
jspektor@email.com

| 12 Highland Avenue | McDonald, PA 15057 | (412) 555–0102 |

EDUCATION:	**Robert Morris University**, Pittsburgh, PA 15108

Bachelor of Arts, Public Relations, 2010
- Dean's List 2008–2010
- Alpha Chi National Scholarship Society member
- Student Vice President for Commuter Affairs

AWARDS: **Telly** (Silver) for "Learning to Work Together," **CINDY** (Finalist), "It's not a ghost, it's real," **New York Festivals** (Finalist) "Me and My Buddy"

COMMUNICATIONS EXERIENCE:

The White House, Washington, D.C.
Intern: Office of the Press Secretary, 2009
- Helped prepare daily press briefings, news releases, and television interviews
- Acted as a liaison between the national press corps and senior White House staff
- Directed journalists' inquiries to the appropriate administration source
- Proofread and edited official documents

RMC-TV, *Public Relations Coordinator*, Robert Morris University, 2008

- Designed and implemented promotional activities
- Wrote grant-winning proposal for national video production
- Started weekly RMC-TV "Studio Notes" column in college newspaper
- Developed advertising campaign to promote new season of programming

Academic Media Center, *Intern,* Robert Morris University, 2007
- Participated in preproduction planning
- Scripted and produced public service announcements for the Pittsburgh Airport Area Chamber of Commerce
- Assistant directed Robert Morris Colonials football broadcasts

Member: Public Relations Society of America

Computer Skills: PC and Macintosh, Microsoft Office, Microsoft Word, Outlook, Quark, Windows, Excel, PowerPoint, Front Page, and PageMaker

REFERENCES AVAILABLE UPON REQUEST

CORPORATE COMMUNICATIONS

Heather Long
3412 Valley Drive
Los Angeles, CA 90024
(310) 555-6554
hjlong@mail.net

EXPERIENCE

Sun Microsystems, Santa Clara, CA, June 2010–August 2010
Intern: Wrote training brochures. Assisted in developing new employee orientation.

Trak Auto, Redwood City, CA, August 2010–Present
Cashier: Answer phones, provide customer service, sell merchandise, stock shelves, and operate register.

Olsten Staffing Service, Palo Alto, CA, 2009–Present
Temporary positions: Answer phone, data entry, photocopy, and other office duties.

Diamond Group, Inc., Mountain View, CA, August 2006–June 2008
Administrative Assistant: Answered phones, filed, typed, computed payroll, prepared paychecks for distribution, created quarterly payroll reports, formulated AIA and invoices for billings, and completed paperwork for worker's compensation and child support.

ACHIEVEMENTS

Palo Alto Transfer Scholarship
Volunteer: Country Meadows Nursing Home
Volunteer: Habitat for Humanity

EDUCATION

San Francisco State College, Bachelor of Science in Communications Management, August 2008–December 2010

Palo Alto Business School, Associate Degree in Business Administration, July 2006–July 2008

REFERENCES AVAILABLE UPON REQUEST

VIDEO ANIMATOR

SCOTT JACKSON

312 Overview Road   East Lansing, MI 48824
(517) 555-2212   scott_r_jackson@email.net

Education

- **Michigan State University**, Bachelor of Science in Communication Mass Media, May 2009

Career-Related Skills

- Computer graphic 3D/2D animation, After Effects compositing and animation, Photoshop/Illustrator design and production

Professional Experience

- **Creative Imaging,** Owner/Operator, 2009–Present: Independent graphics and multimedia servicing. Provides 3D/2D computer animation, rotoscoping, graphic video processing and effects, Web page design, HTML programming, and Photoshop/Illustrator publishing/layout and design for external clients.
- **JPL Productions,** Art Director/Animator, 2008–2009: Responsible for coordinating and creating graphics with both in-house and external clients. Specialized in 3D/2D computer animation, graphic video processing and effects, and layout/design for broadcast television, video, and film.
- **WPMI-TV PBS,** Graphics/Production Technician, 2007–2008: Worked with graphics department providing design for both national and local broadcast programs. Also provided control room and remote graphics support.

Honors and Awards

- **Music Television Networks (MTV)**, 2008: Awarded for an independent music video production entry noted for its graphic video processing and airing nationally.

- **College and Universities Public Relations Association of Michigan Media Award,** 2008: Awarded for an independent video production entry noted for its graphic video processing and special effects.

- **Mass Media Award,** 2004: Presented for an independent student production entitled "Creativity."

Military Experience

- **United States Army Reserves,** New Cumberland Army Depot, New Cumberland, PA, 2002–2005: Headquarters Company, 315th Combat Engineer Group

RADIO

ANTHONY G. CANTINI

(home address)	22 Thompson Road, Erie, PA 16208
	(814) 555-5451
	tonygc78@mail.com
(school address)	1315 N. Broad St., Philadelphia, PA 19122

COMMUNICATIONS EXPERIENCE

WBPA 29, Philadelphia, PA, June 2010–Present
WTWB 19, Johnstown, PA, June 2010–Present
  Master Control Technician/Production Editor: Responsible for on-air programming, satellite feeds, editing, daily maintenance of equipment, and commercial traffic.

WRTI 90.1, Philadelphia, PA, 2008–Present
  Host: *Jazz in the Afternoon.*
  Master of Ceremonies: For remote broadcasts and events.

WHIP, online radio station, Temple University, Philadelphia, PA, 2005–2008
  General Manager: Supervised over 20 volunteers each semester for two years. Strengthened relations with administration. Oversaw reorganization of Executive Board and handled personnel training. Assisted in the following departments: news, music, production, and engineering.

ACTIVITIES

Pittsburgh Irish Festival
  Master of Ceremonies and **Stage Director:** 2009 Irish Festival; 2008 St. Patrick's Day Celebration.
  Assistant Stage Director and **Assistant Sound Technician:** 2007 Irish Festival.

EDUCATION

Temple University, Philadelphia
School of Comunications and Theater, Bachelor of Arts in Media Production, May 2010

Member
  National Association of Radio Broadcasters

References supplied upon request

TELEVISION PRODUCER

Julia Nguyen

239 Lakeside Lane   Memphis, TN 37217
(615) 555-6631   jjnguyen22@email.net

Media *Work Experience*	*Academic Media Center*, University of Memphis (2008–Present): *Various positions* ♦ Station manager of AMC-TV, Channel 10 ♦ Producer and writer of a national video for the Association of College and Universities Housing Officers International ♦ Producer of *Front & Center*, a half-hour movie review program ♦ Coproducer and writer of a regional video for the National Teacher's Training Institute for WQED, Channel 13 ♦ Production assistant for location shoot in Boston, MA, to cover the "Year 2008 Initiative" ♦ Cablecasting supervisor for the 2007 winter semester for Channel 10 ♦ Various crew positions including director, technical director, camera operator, and graphics operator *New Productions*, 501 Baum Boulevard, Memphis, TN 37217 (Summer 2007): *Intern* ♦ Clients included AAA, Idlewild Park, BNAC, and Iron City ♦ Experience in technical operations, location shooting skills, nonlinear editing, and agency-client relationships
Other Work *Experience*	Ray's Clothing & Sporting Goods, Robinson Town Center, Memphis, TN 37217 (2006–Present) *Clothing sales associate* ♦ Assist customers on the sales floor ♦ Merchandise new items onto the sales floor and sign sale items Dairy Queen, Highway 101, Eugene, TN 37307 (2004–2006) *Assistant manager* ♦ Managed all employees on shifts, closed registers and the store ♦ Assisted customers and handled customer problems
Awards and *Honors*	2010 Outstanding Communications Management Student of the Year 2008 Academic Media Center Student of the Year 2007 Who's Who among American Universities and Colleges Repeat Dean's List student
Education	University of Memphis, BS/BA, August 2010 Major: Communications Management, Major GPA: 3.8

References supplied upon request

TEACHING

Keiko Matsumoto-Smith

2485 Alexander Manor   (614) 555-7200
Albion, OH 43952   mskeiko@email.net

Education: Robert Morris University, Pittsburgh, PA, Bachelor of Arts,
English and Communications Education, May 2010, GPA: 3.94
Pennsylvania State Certification in English Education and
Communications (Video Production, Education)

Experience: **Student Teacher**, West Allegheny High School, Fall 2009:
Responsible for creating and delivering curriculum for English
and videography classes. Assumed all planning, grading, and
teaching responsibilities of cooperating teacher. Acquired valuable
presentation and social skills interacting with students, faculty, and
administration. Demonstrated initiative and creativity through the
following projects:
- Created a video scrapbook project for students surrounding
  their participation in President Bush's visit to the area.
- Arranged an interview with a local TV anchor to help students
  learn valuable interviewing techniques.
- Organized a field trip to TV studio.
- Intertwined the use of video in English classrooms by assigning
  students a mini-screenplay based on a short story.
- Used creative resources to teach English students how to write a
  proper business letter.

Business Manager, TVT, Teacher of Television and Video
Consortium, 2009: Organized events for the annual TVT Student
Festival, which included mailing, member contact, and program
coordination. Contributed articles to the TVT newsletter and assisted in publication for distribution.

Master Teacher, NTTI, National Teachers Training Institute,
November 2008: Presented with members of the Robert Morris
University Academic Media Center at Carnegie Science Center in
Pittsburgh, PA. Discussed the value of teaching video production
and the need for technological exposure in the classroom.

Activities: **Western Region Secretary**, Student Pennsylvania State Education
Association
Cocaptain, Robert Morris Cheerleading Squad, 2007–2009
English Student of the Year, 2009
**Alpha Chi Honor Society Academic and Leadership Scholarship
Recipient**

References supplied upon request.

JOURNALISM

Toshia Wells

2700 East 26th Street   651-555-2388
Minneapolis, MN 55406   tcwells85@email.net

Experience

Reporter, *The Bridge* Community Newspaper,
Minneapolis, MN • Summer 2010
- Reported news, conducted interviews, covered neighborhood meetings and business events

Reporter, *Minnesota Spokesman-Recorder*, St. Paul, MN • 2008–2009
- Covered local African American business leaders in monthly profile

Intern, *St. Paul Pioneer Press*, Business Division, St. Paul, MN • Summer 2008
- Reported on local business news and profiled business leaders. Developed feature story on success of Somali entrepreneurs in Twin Cities

Volunteer Work and Activities

Volunteer newspaper adviser, *South High School*, Minneapolis,
MN • Fall 2008–present
- Advise after-school newspaper staff in writing and editing school newspaper

Cellist, *Civic Orchestra of Minneapolis* • 2006–present

Skills

Fluent Spanish. Conversational German and French. HTML. Computer-assisted reporting. Copy editing. Microsoft Office, PhotoShop, PageMaker, and Quark

Education

B.A. in Journalism, *University of Minnesota*: Anticipated May 2011
- Minor in Business Management
- Concentration in Business Writing

Member

American Society of Journalists and Authors

Reference and Clips

Available upon request

SAMPLE COVER LETTERS

September 12, 2010

Toshia Wells
2700 East 26th Street
Minneapolis, MN 55406

Mr. Gideon Applequest
The Springfield Journal
1320 Main Street
Springfield, MN 55408

Dear Mr. Applequest:

I am writing to you as a soon-to-be graduate from the University of Minnesota with extensive business writing experience, ready to start a career in journalism. I have been reading *The Springfield Journal* for years and am confident that my skills and abilities could be useful to this respected newspaper.

For the past year, I worked as a reporter for the *Minnesota Spokesman-Recorder*, where my main responsibility involved writing for the Business Department. I profiled local African American business leaders in a monthly column and covered business-related events throughout the city as well. I also held an internship at the *St. Paul Pioneer Press* during the summer of 2008, where I developed a feature story on the success of Somali entrepreneurs in the Twin Cities. At the *Pioneer Press*, I also learned to juggle reporting with mailroom tasks, photocopying, phone calls, and Internet-based research. My coursework in business management and my mentoring experience with the American Society of Journalists and Authors have also helped to prepare me for a position at *The Springfield Journal.*

I would be honored to work for the state's most widely circulated newspaper, and after three years of reporting and business writing with a variety of area newspapers, I know that I'm ready for the challenges and rewards of working for *The Springfield Journal.*

Attached please find my resumé. I will be happy to provide clips and references upon request. You can reach me by e-mail at tcwells85@email.net or by phone at (651) 555-2388. Thank you for your consideration, and I look forward to hearing from you.

Sincerely,

Toshia Wells

September 15, 2010

Alice Smith
123 Park Ave.
Sarasota, FL 34237

Fred Jones
VP, Programming
Jones Media
123 Street Road
Miami, FL 33131

Dear Mr. Jones:

I am writing to you at the suggestion of Janice Barel. Janice has been my college adviser during my years at Miami University and thought my strong writing skills and willingness to tackle any job might make a good fit with Jones Media. During my past three years of college, I have worked full time for the local cable operator, Comcast Cable, logging tapes and prepping the daily morning show guests.

It's clear from the press releases posted to your Web site that Jones Media is tackling industry trends head-on, including the digital transition, multichannel environments, and cross-platform content development. This is an exciting time to be in the media business, especially with a media company that is involved in many facets of program development. I learn quickly and am able to use what I've learned to develop new ideas and concepts.

I have attached my resumé for your review. Perhaps we could meet in person sometime in early October. I am eager to hear about Jones Media's new programming needs and ways that I might be helpful.

Thank you for your time,

Alice Smith

February 11, 2011

Jonathan Rogers
6462 Laurel Hill Place
Baltimore, MD 21223

Human Resources
Discovery Communications
7700 Wisconsin Avenue
Bethesda, MD 20814

Good morning.

It is with enthusiasm that I reply to your search for an Assistant Producer for The Home Design Show as mentioned on the Discovery Communications jobline. As a producer for a regional college newscast, I am familiar with the deadlines, budgets, and clear vision necessary to execute a weekly magazine-style program. I have consistently worked to ensure that our programs reflect a high production value and respond to key audience demographics.

I am fortunate to have had a wide range of production experiences through internships with several of the local media outlets. I also have experience as an executive producer for the University's end-of-semester show. Executive producing for a cable network with the brand identity and success of Discovery is a special opportunity.

I look forward to speaking with you in person and discussing Discovery's needs and my experience in greater detail. Thank you for your time.

Sincerely,

Jonathan Rogers

Sample Thank-You Notes

June 3, 2011

Latasha Washington
202 14th Street, Apt. 2B
Newark, NJ 07102

Mike Friedman
Brown Dog Online Media
1500 Market Street
New York, NY 10003

Dear Mike:

It's not often I have an opportunity to discuss the cable industry, government regulations, and a recipe for chocolate cake in a single conversation, all before ten o'clock in the morning. Thank you for the eclectic conversation.

Your experiences have confirmed for me what I've heard over and over about Brown Dog Online Media: entrepreneurial gusto is both supported and encouraged. This is a refreshing outlook for any company, let alone one as young as BDOM. It's certainly an enticing characteristic to someone like myself who thrives on new challenges and possibilities.

I hope we'll have an occasion to talk again about the developments you envision for your region. Thank you for your time.

Sincerely,

Latasha Washington

August 25, 2011

David Garles
96 Browning Rd.
Philadelphia, PA 19106

Juan Ramiraz
V.P. Broadcasting
QVC
1334 Executive Parkway
West Chester, PA 19380

Dear Mr. Ramiraz:

Ah, twizzlers—the lunch of sugar-charged television minds everywhere! I guess that explains your overflowing energy, although it does make me wonder about the withdrawal when the jar becomes empty. I need to remember this the next time I enter your office.

Thanks for spending a few minutes with me yesterday. Obviously, productions are going on all the time, and with the recent restructuring I'm sure you need to be in thirty places at once. So I'm grateful for the time we were able to squeeze in. I'm equally grateful for your consideration regarding new positions. As I mentioned when we spoke, based on my previous experience I would be most interested in an entry-level ad sales position.

Your leadership appears to be a real motivating force, and I'd be interested in helping you to fulfill some of your vision in a broader capacity.

Thanks again for your time.

Sincerely,

David Garles

November 16, 2010

Kelly Robb
1113 Susan Dr.
Boston, MA 02108

Karen Lee
Senior Recruiter
MTV Networks
1515 Broadway
New York, NY 10036-5797

Dear Karen:

Thank you for taking the time to meet with me yesterday. I truly enjoyed learning more about the company and its goals for the coming year. After our conversation I followed up on your recommendation that I look into the new John Smith book on the cable industry. From the review I read online it appears to be a book that would definitely enhance my knowledge of the field. I'm looking forward to reading it.

I appreciated your thoughtful questions and attentive listening. Now I understand why Jim Washington felt that talking with you would be a great next step. Ideally, there will be a place within MTV Networks where your needs and my experience will be a perfect fit.

I look forward to speaking with you next week and meeting with the other folks you recommended.

Again, thank you for your time.

Sincerely,

Kelly Robb

CONCLUSION

Let's assume at this point that you've read the preceding chapters and you're still passionate about finding a job in the media and communications field. Before starting your career search, we have a few more pieces of advice. First, if you want to work in this field—really want to—then go after it with gusto. But don't compare your path to your friends' paths or to a path taken by the person featured in the alumni newsletter or by the manager featured in the industry-insider magazine. Everyone's path is different, and people with seemingly divergent career paths can end up in similar jobs years down the line. The key is to know the path that is right for you.

For some, starting with an entry-level job in the company of their dreams is the right path. If working for Google or MTV or NBC is your dream, then get your foot in the door with a job in any department. A benefit of this approach is that companies often promote from within. Once you're in the company, you're likely to hear about job openings before people on the outside do, and you may even meet people within the company who are willing to introduce you to the "right" people in other divisions. The challenge with this approach is that this entry-level position might not be in your preferred area. For example, you might find an entry-level position in the news division when your interest really lies with the online division. For this approach to work, however, you must give 110 percent to the position in which you're placed. Otherwise, word of your lack of motivation will get around, and you'll be unlikely to find others willing to help you move up the ladder.

Another approach is to seek out the type of work or position that you desire in a small company or in a small market. The advantage with this approach is that you'll gain skills in the area in which you most want to work. Once you gather some experience, you can decide whether you want to move to a larger market or company, or stay in a smaller market—a choice often made for quality-of-life reasons. However, working in a smaller market or organization often means that you will have to move from company to company in order to gain responsibility.

Both approaches can work. You might even try both and be willing to take either type of position. But when you land in one or the other, go back and read the paragraphs above. Those words of guidance can help you make the best of either opportunity. Both paths offer opportunities if you're willing to seize them.

Second, consider all the possibilities. There are many media career opportunities other than those found within actual media companies. Corporate communications, government agencies, and even training and development companies complete billions of dollars' worth of communications work annually. Consider the video game industry or any of the new media companies supplying Internet communications, including phone companies. Consider areas that are experiencing high growth—graphic animation, public relations, or social media. These are all worth exploring.

In addition, the recent trend of media consolidation means that a single media conglomerate might provide access to numerous other media companies. For example, if you get a job at a local NBC affiliate, you're instantly connected to the NBC national network. In addition, since NBC, as of the printing of this edition, is soon to be owned by Comcast, you'll be connected to a wide variety of Comcast-owned media companies, including MSNBC, The Golf Channel, PBS Kids Sprout, Court TV, Bravo, even the Philadelphia 76ers basketball team. Similar connections can be found at every major television network and most other large media companies.

A third productive way to job hunt is to start with location. Whether you're moving to a new place or looking for a job in your hometown, it's worth calling the mayor's office or the local Chamber of Commerce or visiting the Web sites of local search firms. These organizations can send you information packets or give you ideas over the phone about local businesses involved in media and communications. If you have contacts in a geographic area, call or write those people to schedule informational interviews. Don't assume that they know your interests or already know that you're looking for a job. Treat these contacts professionally, and they will do the same for you. They might even know which companies are hiring. By starting with location, you can proceed in a logical, thorough manner. This strategy can help focus your search and may turn up new opportunities to explore.

Finally, we cannot stress enough that proper preparation is the secret to a successful job search. We have seen it pay off for many, many people. There is intense competition for the best jobs, and preparing yourself while in college is the first step toward success. So get started!

ADDITIONAL RESOURCES

American Salaries and Wages Survey. 9th ed. New York: Gale Group, 2007.

Anthony, Mitchell. *Creating Success: Interviews with Successful People.* http://www.creatingsuccesspodcast.com.

Bennett, Scott. *The Elements of Résumé Style: Essential Rules and Eye-Opening Advice for Writing Résumés and Cover Letters That Work.* New York: American Management Association, 2005.

Bolles, Richard Nelson. *What Color Is Your Parachute? 2009: A Practical Manual for Job-Hunters and Career Changers.* Berkeley, CA: Ten Speed Press, 2008. http://www.jobhuntersbible.com.

Camerson, Blythe. *Great Jobs for Communication Majors.* New York: McGraw-Hill, 2001.

Carter, Carol. *Majoring in the Rest of Your Life: Career Secrets for College Students.* Denver, CO: Lifebound, 2004.

Darga, Amy, ed. *Job Hunter's Sourcebook: Where to Find Employment Leads and Other Job Search Resources.* 8th ed. New York: Gale Research, 2008.

Donovan, Craig P., and Jim Garnett. *Internships for Dummies.* New York: Hungry Minds, 2001.

Drapes, Michaela. *Vault Guide to the Top Media and Entertainment Employers.* New York: Vault, 2008.

Enelow, Wendy S., and Louise Kursmark. *Cover Letter Magic.* 3rd ed. Indianapolis, IN: Jist Works, 2006.

Fry, Ron. *Your First Resume: For Students and Anyone Preparing to Enter Today's Tough Job Market.* New York: Career Press, 2001.

Gardner, Philip, ed. *Recruiting Trends 2007–2008.* East Lansing, MI: Institutional Media Center, Michigan State University, 2008.

Hamedeh, Samer, and Mark Oldman. *Vault Guide to Top Internships, 2008 edition.* New York: Vault, 2008.

Hedrick, Tom, Mike McKenzie, and Joe Castiglione. *The Art of Sportscasting: How to Build a Successful Career.* South Bend, IN: Diamond Communications, 2000.

Lieber, Ron, and Tom Meltzer. *Best Entry Level Jobs, 2008 Edition.* New York: Princeton Review, 2007.

Nadler, Burton Jay. *The Everything Cover Letter Book: Great Cover Letters for Everybody from Student to Executive.* Holbrook, MA: Adams Media Corporation, 2005.

Noronha, Shonan. *Careers in Communication.* 4th ed. New York: McGraw-Hill, 2004.

Oldman, Mark, and Samer Hamedeh. *Internship Bible.* 10th ed. New York: Princeton Review, 2005.

Taylor, Allan, and James Robert Parish. *Career Opportunities in Television and Cable.* New York: Facts on File, 2006.

U.S. Bureau of Labor Statistics. *The Occupational Outlook Handbook, 2008–2009 Edition.* http://www.bls.gov/OCO.

U.S. Bureau of Labor Statistics. *Occupational Projections and Training Data, 2008–2009 Edition.* http://www.bls.gov/emp/optd.

Weddle, Peter. *2009/10 Guide to Employment Sites on the Internet.* 10th ed. Stamford, CT: Weddle's, 2009.

Whitcomb, Susan Britton. *Résumé Magic.* Indianapolis, IN: Jist Works, 2006.

INDEX